Diversity Business Alignment Maps

Utilizing Intangible Human Capital Assets to Produce Tangible Business Results

Dr. Edward E. Hubbard, Ph.D.

D-BAM: Diversity Business Alignment Maps

Diversity Business Alignment Maps: Utilizing Intangible Human Capital Assets to Produce Tangible Business Results

Copyright © 2017 by Dr. Edward E. Hubbard, Ph.D.

All rights reserved. The reproduction or utilization of this work in any form or by any electronic, mechanical or other means, known now or hereafter invented, including xerography, photocopying and recording and in any information storage and retrieval system, is forbidden without the written permission of Hubbard & Hubbard, Inc. This manual may not be changed or reprinted in any other form without written permission of the publisher. Printed in the United States of America.

ISBN 978-1-883733-32-2

GLOBAL
INSIGHTS
PUBLISHING

832 Garfield Drive, Petaluma, CA 94954
Office: (707)763-8380 Fax:(435)674-1203

Preface

Your boss just told you for your Diversity and Inclusion (D&I) organization to truly deliver what the C-Suite wants and remain viable, you need to "think more strategically". You want your D&I organization to be successful however you are puzzled by your boss's statement. What does *that* mean? You thought you were being "strategic". Now, you are not so sure what you are doing will keep your efforts in the "value-added" column and off the budget cutting or elimination table.

In the pages that follow, we'll take a closer look at several key aspects of strategy and thinking strategically... identifying what it is, why it's important, who needs to think strategically, what distinguishes strategic thinkers, and what the steps are in the strategic thinking process. We will also explore how strategic thinking skills are essential to create a series of strategic execution models called "D-BAMs" or Diversity Business Alignment Maps that drive measurable business performance outcomes linked to the bottom-line.

In **Chapter One** you will find an introduction explaining the strategic importance of strategy and what it means to think and operate strategically. We will explore what characteristics set Diversity and Inclusion strategic thinkers above the rest. We will also examine the definition of "Strategy Maps" and "D-BAMs"

D-BAM: Diversity Business Alignment Maps

and how they are used to drive organizational performance and success.

Chapter Two revisits the Business Case for Diversity and Inclusion, however in this review we will focus on what the C-Suite wants from its Diversity and Inclusion efforts thru the lens of a Diversity Business Alignment Map (D-BAM). We will explore how intangible assets like Diversity and Inclusion can generate tangible benefits. This chapter outlines how Diversity and Inclusion can serve as a major competitive and strategic advantage in the organization's marketplace and how costly it can be when Diversity and Inclusion "performance sciences" **ARE NOT** used.

Chapter Three provides a detailed look at how to build a Diversity Business Alignment Map to tell your Impact Story. It highlights critical steps you can take to forge a strategic business partner alignment with the organization's goals and objectives.

Chapter Four explains the "Value Creation" process and how to deploy the D-BAM strategy enterprise-wide with an effective D&I ROI measurement-based approach.

Chapter Five highlights detailed steps to "align" the Diversity and Inclusion strategy to create measurable strategic value. It provides key considerations to integrate the D-BAM strategy into the organization's operating network. The chapter reviews six objectives that consistently appear in strategy maps that are crucial

D-BAM: Diversity Business Alignment Maps

for success. It outlines the key levels of analysis that are mandatory for generating a Diversity ROI payoff and impact. Accountability components are discussed as well as incentive structures to drive key map-performance outcome behaviors.

Chapter Six lays out a roadmap to ensure that culture and climate supports the successful execution of the D-BAM strategy. This segment helps examine the "fit" between culture and the D-BAM strategy along with recommendations and techniques to re-align the process. Instructions to navigate the path of politics and influence are explained and suggestions for improving network support are discussed.

Chapter Seven explores the benefits received by using the D-BAM methodology to communicate with the C-Suite and other key stakeholders. It highlights the skill enhancement and credibility upgrades Diversity and Inclusion practitioners can gain by using the combined "science-based" processes, tools, worksheets, templates, mapping strategies, and more. The use of these tools result in the Diversity and Inclusion professional exhibiting a business competency approach to contribute to the organization's success.

Chapter Eight rounds out the D-BAM discussion and implementation strategy with "time-tested" and "field-proven" tools you can use immediately that are designed to support the

D-BAM: Diversity Business Alignment Maps

implementation of a well-executed D-BAM strategy. They are built to help you make a measurable improvement difference on the organizations' bottom-line.

Acknowledgements

My first and deepest appreciation goes to my wonderful, caring wife, Myra. You are truly my friend, soul-mate and my rock. God Blessed me tremendously with such a beautiful person, inside and out. You constantly give me inspiration and support to continue to do this work. You complete me.

Secondly, I would like to thank my wonderful family. First, to my mother, Geneva Hubbard (in memoriam) whose love and strong foundation-setting values always keeps me strong. You left me with so many wonderful memories and guidelines to live by I will always treasure.

To my sons, Chance and Ed II, to my Grandson, Jamil, whose blueprint for life is still under construction but developing rapidly, what a precious gift from God. To Sarah Holmberg (who is so close I feel she is the daughter I never had) and Jimmy, Sarah's soul-mate. To my sisters Leona, Lois, Sylvia, Jan, Debbie, and their families, my nieces and nephews, especially my nephew and niece Darrel and Rocki Branch, and niece Camille. You truly show your love and caring in so many ways. To Emilio Egea and Pastor Shane Wallis whom I can always count on to have my back when I need it most. Thank you for your authentic love and support. To Roy and Suzanne, along with Darrel and Rocki who open their home and always treat us with fun and stimulating conversation at

D-BAM: Diversity Business Alignment Maps

the beginning of each year so that Myra and I can recharge and keep going. And to a host of other relatives and friends who always keep us in their prayers.

To our extended family Sheila and Phillip Parks, Berto and their families. You have always been there for us with genuine love, friendship and support, especially during our crazy schedules. To Pastors Ron and Monica Hunt for your friendship, love and support, and our church families, as well as many others too numerous to list…Thank You. I appreciate the gift of sharing your love, spirit, and insights. I am forever grateful. May God continue to Bless you with all that life has to offer.

Ed

October, 2017

Table of Contents

Diversity Business Alignment Maps 1
    Utilizing Intangible Human Capital Assets to Produce Tangible Business Results 1

Diversity Business Alignment Maps: Utilizing Intangible Human Capital Assets to Produce Tangible Business Results ..2

    Preface 3

    Acknowledgements 7

    Table of Contents 9

    Chapter One: The Importance of Strategy 15

        What is "Strategy" and "Strategic Thinking"? 16

        Who Needs to Think Strategically? 17

        What Characteristics Set Diversity and Inclusion Strategic Thinkers above the Rest? 19

        What are the Steps in Strategic Thinking? 21

        What are "Strategy Maps?" 23

            The Human Capital – Intangibles Connection 25

            Intangible Assets 30

        Building and Implementing "Solution-Centered" Diversity Strategies 32

        Financial Planning versus Strategic Planning 33

        STRATEGY IS A STEP IN A CONTINUUM 43

        What are "Diversity Business Alignment Maps (D-BAM)?" 45

D-BAM: Diversity Business Alignment Maps

References 50

Chapter Two: The Business Case for Diversity 53

A Diversity Measurement Challenge: How Can We Ensure that Diversity Is "at" the Strategic Business Table, Not "on" the Menu? 53

Can a Perceived Intangible Asset Like Diversity Generate Tangible Benefits? 57

Diversity Facts, Figures, and Financial Performance 62

What Do We Mean by Diversity? 64

Diversity Provides a Business Advantage 67

Failure to Implement a Diversity Initiative Can Be Costly . 73

Diversity Links to Productivity and Performance 75

Retention 77

Productivity 79

The Link Between the Lack of Diversity Programs and Absenteeism 82

Diversity's Contribution to the Bottom Line 84

Building Centers of Diversity Excellence 87

Final Thoughts 96

References 96

Chapter Three: Building a Diversity D-BAM to Tell Your Impact Story 99

The Power of Diversity ROI (DROI®) Measurement Alignment 99

What Is Top Management Support? 102

How Do You Begin the Alignment Process? 104

D-BAM: Diversity Business Alignment Maps

Step 1: Start Thinking of Diversity and Inclusion Metrics as a Critical Part of the Business. 105

Step 2: Learn the Business! 105

Step 3: Develop Measurement Strategies and Activities That Line Managers Want. 106

Step 4: Involve Top Management. 107

Step 5: Develop Interventions that are Practical, How-To Approaches 107

Step 6: Get a Handle on Diversity R.O.I. (DROI®) 109

How Are Diversity Training Analysis and Evaluation Linked to Diversity Measurement Alignment? 116

References 119

Chapter Four: The Value Creation Process 121

Creating Value Enterprise-wide 121

Make Measurement Follow Initiatives 126

Experience of Inclusion.. 127

Hubbard Inclusion ROI Metrics 128

Importance of Strategic Diversity ROI Measurement and Value Creation 131

Creating the Proper Measurement Environment for Success 135

References 140

Chapter Five: Aligning Intangible Assets to Business Strategy 141

Alignment: Intangible Assets Must Be Aligned with Strategy in Order to Create Value. 141

Integration 142

D-BAM: Diversity Business Alignment Maps

Human Capital 144
Information Capital 144
Organization Capital 144
The Importance of Business Alignment 146
Determining the Payoff Needs 149
Creating a Strategic Link 153

    Senior Management' Overall Role, Responsibilities, and Critical Accountabilities that Drive Performance 154

    Principal Responsibilities and Activities 154

        Establishing Vision and Strategies 154

        Allocating Resources 155

        Establishing Accountability 155

        Modeling Diversity and Inclusion Leadership Behavior 156

        Putting Principles into Practice 156

        Communication and Education Programs 159

        Goal-Setting Programs 160

        Reward System Linkage 160

    Motivating outstanding performance to achieve the strategic, financial, Diversity and Inclusion climate, and operational goals of the organization. 160

    Provide key managers an opportunity to directly share in the benefits of outstanding Diversity and Inclusion climate, operating and financial performance. 160

    Provide focus on particular areas of organizational concern and reward performance in those areas. 161

D-BAM: Diversity Business Alignment Maps

Communicating With the Board of Directors and External Shareholders 165

Reward Systems Linkage 166

Final Thoughts 170

References 171

Further Readings 173

Chapter Six: Creating the Strategy-focused Diversity Organization 175

Building a Strategy-Supportive Corporate Culture 179

What Is Organizational and Corporate Culture? 181

Manifestations of Culture 182

Creating the fit between Strategy and Culture 187

Symbolic Actions and Substantive Actions 188

Building a Spirit of High Performance into the Culture 191

Fostering a Strategy-Supportive Climate and Culture 196

Keeping the Internal Organization Responsive and Innovative 199

Fostering Champions 201

Dealing with Company Politics 202

References 207

Chapter Seven: Using a D-BAM to Become an Evidence-based Diversity & Inclusion Professional 211

Art versus Science 212

Checking Your Ingredients for Success 214

References 225

D-BAM: Diversity Business Alignment Maps

Chapter Eight: 227
A Few D-BAM Action Tools You Can Use 227
About the Author 237
    A Brief Bio 237
Other Resources 241
    Diversity ROI Certification Institutes and Training 241
    Hubbard Diversity ROI Institute 241
    Earn Six Professional Certifications in Diversity ROI - Available ONLY from Hubbard & Hubbard, Inc. 242
    Hubbard Diversity Measurement & Productivity Institute 245
    Professional Competency-based Training and Skill-building 245
    Hubbard & Hubbard, Inc. Products and Services 245
    Products Web 245
    Hubbard ERG and BRG ROI Institute 246
    ERG and BRG Training, Skill-building, and ROI Measurement Techniques for Resource Group Leaders, Sponsors, and Members 246
    Metriclink Dashboard and Scorecard Services 247
    Comprehensive Online Performance Measurement and Management Services for Organizational Excellence 247
    Performance Spotlights and Publishing Opportunities 248
    Measuring ROI of Diversity Initiatives, ERG/BRG Initiatives, and Other Webinars 249
Index 251

Chapter One: The Importance of Strategy

Your boss just told you for your Diversity and Inclusion (D&I) organization to truly deliver what the C-Suite wants and remain viable, you need to "think more strategically". You want your D&I organization to be successful however you are puzzled by your boss's statement. What does *that* mean? You thought you were being "strategic". Now, you are not so sure what you are doing will keep your efforts in the "value-added" column and off the budget cutting or elimination table.

In the pages that follow, we'll take a closer look at several key aspects of strategy and thinking strategically… identifying what it is, why it's important, who needs to think strategically, what distinguishes strategic thinkers, and what the steps are in the strategic thinking process. We will also explore how strategic thinking skills are essential to create a series of strategic execution models called "D-BAMs" or Diversity Business Alignment Maps that drive measurable business performance outcomes linked to the bottom-line.

What is "Strategy" and "Strategic Thinking"?

In its most basic sense from a Diversity and Inclusion point of view, "strategy" **can be defined as the "unique and sustainable ways by which the Diversity and Inclusion organization creates value"**. Strategic thinking, on the other hand, is about **"analyzing opportunities and problems from a broad perspective and understanding the potential impact your actions using Diversity and Inclusion as a performance improvement strategy might have on the organization and others"**. Strategic thinkers visualize what might or could be, and take a holistic approach to day-to-day issues and challenges. And they make this an ongoing process rather than a onetime event. "Utilizing strategy" that is Diversity and Inclusion-focused, consists of **using unique and sustainable ways to apply diverse human capital assets of the organization in a deliberate, measurable way to drive value throughout and directly to the organizations' bottom-line**.

Like other Diversity & Inclusion managers, or any manager for that matter, you will routinely encounter complex situations, difficult problems, and challenging decisions. Your job is to deal with these situations as best you can by using the information you have. In an ideal world, you would have access to all the information you need to navigate through these challenges. Unavoidably, however, you have only a limited amount of

D-BAM: Diversity Business Alignment Maps

information to work with. And because you sit in a particular part of your organization, you have a limited view of the forces that lie outside your sphere of influence.

Strategic thinking also nets you valuable professional and personal benefits including the respect and appreciation of your boss, peers, and direct reports.

Who Needs to Think Strategically?

In today's highly competitive and fast-changing business world, *everyone* in an organization must know how to think strategically. Only then can an organization leverage the full range of creativity and knowledge embodied throughout its diverse workforce. Strategic thinking can be especially effective when it's done collaboratively as well as individually. By thinking strategically working in diverse groups, employees gain other people's perspectives on critical and complex issues which are important benefits in today's challenging business landscape. Every manager in your organization has a unique view of how the company operates. As the expert in applying Diversity and Inclusion performance solutions, you must personally master the ability to thinks strategically and use it often in your role as a skilled Diversity and Inclusion professional. In addition, you must encourage managers to incorporate this skill in their day-to-day work by asking a diverse group of peer managers' questions about

D-BAM: Diversity Business Alignment Maps

how they interact with people from various parts of the organization; you strengthen their understanding regarding how their actions might affect their work and the work of others.

For instance, suppose the manager works in accounts receivable and want to overhaul the billing system. You know that the IT group, as well as all managers who generate bills, will be affected. So you encourage the manager to ask a diverse group of others in the organization about how changing the billing system might have an impact on them. Through conversations with people in the marketing department, the manager learns that his/her proposed changes will have significant consequences for the package design group. Why? All designs will now need to incorporate a larger barcode to accommodate changes in the billing-system technology. By using your knowledge of the power of collaborating with others with diverse perspectives, you help the manager gain greater insight into the complex ramifications of even seemingly minor decisions. This insight, in turn, helps him/her make more strategic choices. As we will learn later, this type of strategic thinking is essential and a common element in building a Diversity Business Alignment Map (D-BAM).

D-BAM: Diversity Business Alignment Maps

What Characteristics Set Diversity and Inclusion Strategic Thinkers above the Rest?

Diversity & Inclusion professionals who think strategically demonstrate specific personal traits, behaviors, attitudes, and thinking skills. For example, you're on your way to becoming a strategic thinker if you exhibit the following *personal traits:*

- **Curiosity.** You're genuinely interested in what's going on in business units, company, industry, and wider business environment. You're curious about others who are different.
- **Flexibility.** You're able to adapt approaches and shift ideas when new information suggests the need to do so.
- **Future focus.** You constantly consider how the conditions in which your group and company operate may change in the coming months and years. And you keep an eye out for opportunities that may prove valuable in the future as well threats that may be looming.
- **Positive outlook.** You view challenges as opportunities, and you believe that success is possible.
- **Openness.** *You* welcome new ideas from supervisors, peers, employees, and outside stakeholders such as customers, suppliers, and business partners. *You* also take criticism well by not reacting in a defensive manner.
- **Breadth.** *You* continually work to broaden your knowledge and experience, so you can see connections and patterns across seemingly unrelated fields of knowledge. *You* have the makings of a strategic thinker if

D-BAM: Diversity Business Alignment Maps

you continually anticipate your actions' impact on a wide range of individuals including, but not limited to, your boss, direct reports, peers, and customers.

To do this, you need to demonstrate the following *behaviors:*

- Seek other people's opinions.
- Ask questions and challenge assumptions about how the world works.
- Focus on the future.
- Identify the forces driving your unit's and company's performance and think about how to improve that performance.
- Watch the competition.
- Reassess who your customers are and what they value.
- Stay up to date on developments occurring in your unit, in other groups in the company, and in your industry overall.
- Open yourself to ongoing learning by reading books, magazines' and industry reports; attending seminars; and talking with experts.

By practicing these behaviors, you more readily spot valuable new opportunities to capitalize on. And you identify and repel potential threats before they can do any real damage. Finally, Diversity & Inclusion strategic thinkers demonstrate characteristic *thinking skills.* They:

- Objectively analyze a situation and evaluate the pros, cons, and implications of any course of action.

D-BAM: Diversity Business Alignment Maps

- Grasp abstract ideas and put the "pieces" together to form a coherent picture.
- Generate a wide range of options, visualize new possibilities, and formulate fresh approaches to their work.
- Factor hunches into their decision making without allowing their hunches to dominate the final outcome.
- Understand the cause-and-effect linkages among the many elements that create a system whether the system is their team, unit, or organization, or a project or process.

What are the Steps in Strategic Thinking?

Strategic thinking can be broken down into two phases, each of which consists of specific steps.

Phase 1: setting the stage consists of two steps:

1. **Seeing the big picture** - understanding the broader business environment in which you operate.

2. **Articulating strategic objectives** - determining what you hope to achieve by thinking strategically.

Phase 2 applying your skills consists of five additional steps:

3. **Identifying relationships, patterns, and trends** - spotting patterns across seemingly unrelated events, and categorizing

D-BAM: Diversity Business Alignment Maps

related information to reduce the number of issues you must grapple with at one time.

4. **Getting creative** - generating alternatives, visualizing new possibilities, challenging your assumptions, and opening yourself to new information.

5. **Analyzing information** - sorting out and prioritizing the most important information while making a decision, managing a project, handling a conflict, and so forth.

6. **Prioritizing your actions** - staying focused on your objectives while handling multiple demands and competing priorities.

7. **Making trade-offs** - recognizing the potential advantages and disadvantages of an idea **or** course of action, making choices regarding what you will and won't do, and balancing short- and long-term concerns.

The characteristics of Diversity and Inclusion strategic thinkers along with their efforts to build skills to master the steps to incorporate strategic thinking in the Diversity and Inclusion work provides the foundation to translate the organization's strategy and the Diversity and Inclusion strategy into operational terms. This process integration serves as a major cornerstone to effectively demonstrate Diversity and Inclusion's impact on the bottom-line.

D-BAM: Diversity Business Alignment Maps

Before we go much further, let's take a moment to define the term "Strategy Map" and review the definition of a "D-BAM".

What are "Strategy Maps?"

During their seminal work, which led to the application of a "Balanced Scorecard", Drs. Robert S. Kaplan and David P. Norton learned to start each client engagement by getting executives to agree on word statements of their objectives in the four Balanced Scorecard (BSC) perspectives (Financial, Customer, Internal, Learning and Growth). Once the executives agreed to the word statements stating what they wanted to accomplish—how they wanted to describe success—the selection of measurements became much simpler. And, in an interesting twist, the selection of measures became somewhat less consequential. After all, when agreement existed about the objective to be achieved, even if the initial measurements for the objective turned out to be less than perfect, the executives could easily modify the measurements for subsequent periods, without having to redo their discussion about strategy. The objectives would likely remain the same even as the measurements of the objectives evolved with experience and new data sources.

The focus on objectives led to a breakthrough: Objectives should be linked in cause-and-effect relationships. Executives, as they listed objectives in the four perspectives, instinctively started to

D-BAM: Diversity Business Alignment Maps

draw arrows to link the objectives. They could now articulate their strategy demonstrating how improving employee capabilities and skills in certain job positions, coupled with new technology, would enable a critical internal process to improve. The improved process would enhance the value proposition delivered to targeted customers, leading to increased customer satisfaction, retention, and growth in customers' businesses. The improved customer outcome measures would then lead to increased revenues and ultimately significantly higher shareholder value.

Soon they were coaching all the executive teams to describe their strategy by explicit cause-and-effect relationships among the objectives in the four BSC perspectives. Drs. Kaplan and Norton called this diagram a *"strategy map"*. And while every organization's strategy map was different, reflecting their different industries and strategies, they could, after facilitating the development of hundreds of strategy maps, see a basic pattern emerge. They formulated a generic strategy map to serve as a starting point for any organization in any industry (discussed in detail later in this book). The strategy map has turned out to be as important an innovation as the original Balanced Scorecard itself. Executives find the visual representation of strategy both natural and powerful.

D-BAM: Diversity Business Alignment Maps

The Human Capital – Intangibles Connection

Companies can now focus their human capital investments and, more generally, their investments in all intangible assets to create distinctive and sustainable value. All organizations today create sustainable value from leveraging their intangible assets—human capital; databases and information systems; responsive, high-quality processes; customer relationships and brands; innovation capabilities; and culture. The trend away from a product-driven economy, based on tangible assets, to knowledge and service economies, based on intangible assets, has been occurring for decades.

"*Strategy*" describes how an organization intends to create sustained value for its shareholders. Organizations today must leverage their intangible assets for sustainable value creation. Creating value from intangible assets differs in several important ways from creating value by managing tangible physical and financial assets:

Value creation is indirect. Intangible assets such as knowledge and technology seldom have a direct impact on financial outcomes such as increased revenues, lowered costs, and higher profits. It is the "utilization of and improvements in intangible assets that affect financial outcomes through chains of cause-and-effect relationships which can be viewed and understood as a *"chain of impact"*.

D-BAM: Diversity Business Alignment Maps

For example, employee training in LEAN and other six sigma techniques can directly improve process quality. Such improvement can then be expected to lead to improved customer satisfaction, which, in turn, should increase customer loyalty. Ultimately, customer loyalty leads to improved sales and margins from long-term customer relationships.

Value is contextual. The value of an intangible asset depends on its alignment with the strategy. Training employees in LEAN and six sigma techniques has greater value for organizations following a low total cost strategy than for one following a product leadership and innovation strategy.

Value is potential. The cost of investing in an intangible asset represents a poor estimate of its value to the organization. Intangible assets, like employees trained in statistical quality control and root cause analysis, have potential value but not market value. Internal processes such as design, production, delivery, and customer service are required to transform the potential value of intangible assets into tangible value. If the internal processes are not directed at the customer value proposition or financial improvements, then the potential value of employee capabilities and intangible assets in general, will not be realized.

Assets are bundled. Intangible assets seldom create value by themselves. They do not have a value that can be isolated from organizational context and strategy. The value from intangible

D-BAM: Diversity Business Alignment Maps

assets arises when they are combined effectively with other assets, both tangible and intangible. For example, quality training is enhanced when employees have access to timely, detailed data from process-oriented information systems. Maximum value is created when all the organization's intangible assets are aligned with each other, with the organization's tangible assets, and with the strategy.

The Balanced Scorecard strategy map below provides a framework to illustrate how strategy links intangible assets to value-creating processes.

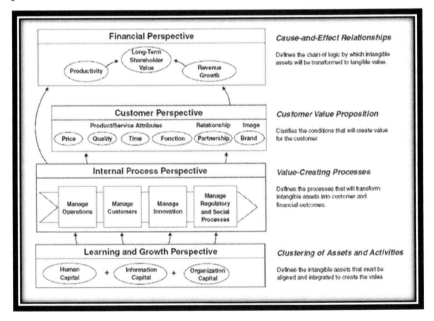

Linking Intangibles to Value Creation

Kaplan, Robert S.; Norton, David P.. Strategy Maps: Converting Intangible Assets into Tangible Outcomes (Kindle Locations 671-672). Harvard Business Review Press. Kindle Edition.

D-BAM: Diversity Business Alignment Maps

The financial perspective describes the tangible outcomes of the strategy in traditional financial terms. Measures such as ROI, shareholder value, profitability, revenue growth, and cost per unit are the lag indicators that show whether the organization's strategy is succeeding or failing. The customer perspective defines the value proposition for targeted customers. The value proposition provides the context for the intangible assets to create value. If customers value consistent quality and timely delivery, then the skills, systems, and processes that produce and deliver quality products and services are highly valuable to the organization. If the customer values innovation and high performance, then the skills, systems, and processes that create new products and services with superior functionality take on high value. Consistent alignment of actions and capabilities with the customer value proposition is the core of strategy execution. The financial and customer perspectives describe the desired outcomes from the strategy. Both perspectives contain many lag indicators. How does the organization create these desired outcomes? The internal process perspective identifies the critical few processes that are expected to have the greatest impact on the strategy.

For example, one organization may increase its internal R&D investments and reengineer its product development processes so that it can develop high-performance, innovative products for its customers. Another organization, attempting to deliver the same

D-BAM: Diversity Business Alignment Maps

value proposition, might choose to develop new products through joint-venture product partnerships.

The learning and growth perspective identifies the intangible assets that are most important to the strategy. The objectives in this perspective identify which jobs (the human capital), which systems (the information capital), and what kind of climate and culture (the organization capital) are required to support the value-creating internal processes. These assets must be bundled together and aligned to the critical internal processes. The objectives in the four perspectives are linked together by cause-and-effect relationships.

Starting from the top is the hypothesis that financial outcomes can be achieved only if targeted customers are satisfied. The customer value proposition describes how to generate sales and loyalty from targeted customers. The internal processes create and deliver the customer value proposition. And intangible assets that support the internal processes provide the foundation for the strategy. Aligning objectives in these four perspectives is the key to value creation and, hence, to a focused and internally consistent strategy. This architecture of cause and effect, linking the four perspectives, is the structure around which a strategy map is developed. Building a strategy map forces an organization to clarify the logic of how it will create value and for whom.

D-BAM: Diversity Business Alignment Maps

Intangible Assets

The dictionary definition of intangible, "incapable of being realized or defined", points to the difficulty that an organization has in managing these assets. How can it manage what can't be defined?

The learning and growth perspective of the Balanced Scorecard highlights the role for aligning the organization's intangible assets to its strategy (see Figure below):

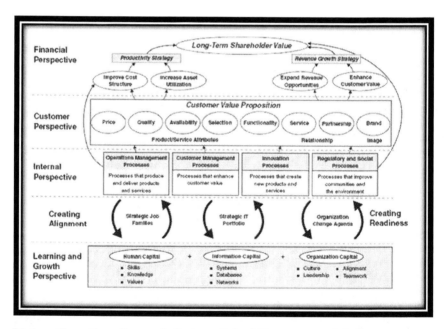

Value Creation through Intangible Alignment with Strategy

Kaplan, Robert S.; Norton, David P.. Strategy Maps: Converting Intangible Assets into Tangible Outcomes (Kindle Location 3170). Harvard Business Review Press. Kindle Edition.

D-BAM: Diversity Business Alignment Maps

This perspective contains the objectives and measures for three components of intangible assets essential for implementing any strategy:

- Human Capital
- Information Capital, and
- Organization Capital

The objectives in these three components must be aligned with the objectives for the internal processes and integrated with each other. Intangible assets should build upon the capabilities created in other intangible and tangible assets, rather than create independent capabilities with no synergies among them.

Objectives should be linked in cause-and-effect relationships to demonstrate how Diversity & Inclusion initiatives can drive organizational performance. I created Diversity Business Alignment Maps to provide Diversity and Inclusion Professionals with the ability to display this linkage to the organization's business strategy directly.

This 3-component framework and philosophy is a required and standard convention when building Diversity Business Alignment Maps (D-BAMs). The D-BAM below reflects the same principle as a means to help drive Diversity and Inclusion value for the organization using "alignment" and "creating readiness".

D-BAM: Diversity Business Alignment Maps

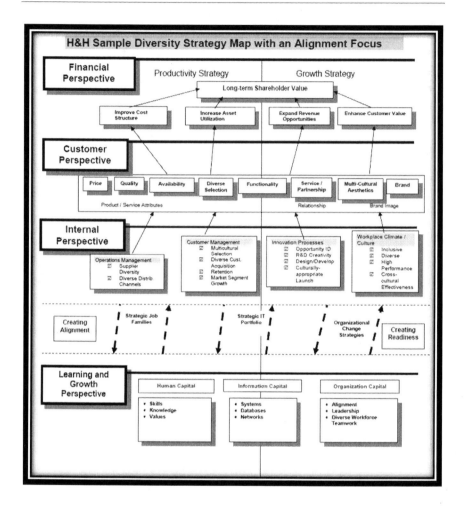

Building and Implementing "Solution-Centered" Diversity Strategies

Michael Porter argues that "the essence of strategy is in the activities—choosing to perform activities differently or to perform different activities than rivals." He observed that: Strategic fit among many activities is fundamental not only to competitive advantage but also to the sustainability of that advantage. It is

D-BAM: Diversity Business Alignment Maps

harder for a rival to match an array of interlocked activities than it is merely to imitate a particular sales-force approach, match a process technology, or replicate a set of product features. Positions built on systems of activities are far more sustainable than those built on individual activities.

Organizations' strategy maps should follow this prescription. The strategic objectives in the internal process and learning and growth perspectives cannot be individually optimized. They must be integrated and aligned to deliver the value proposition underlying the organization's strategy. In this chapter, we illustrate the process for several generic strategies. Of course, for any particular application, the organization must adapt and customize these generic strategy maps to its unique situation.

Financial Planning versus Strategic Planning

Do you need a financial plan? Call any of the major accounting firms and ask for their assistance. The results they deliver will be strikingly similar. Each plan will have a pro forma income statement, balance sheet, cash flow forecast, and capital plan. The actual contents of the plans may differ, based on the knowledge and experience of the accountant, but the structure will be the same.

Look how this situation changes when you need a strategic plan. You can go to any of the major strategy consulting firms for help,

D-BAM: Diversity Business Alignment Maps

but the results they deliver will not be similar in any way. One firm will look at your portfolio of businesses. Another will focus on processes. A third may analyze customer segments and value propositions. Others will stress shareholder value, core competencies, e-strategy, or change management. Unlike financial management, strategy has no generally accepted definitions or framework. There are as many definitions of strategy as there are strategy gurus.

Why is this situation a problem? In this era of diverse knowledge workers, strategy must be executed at all levels of the organization. People must change their behaviors and adopt new values. The key to this transformation is putting strategy at the center of the management process. Strategy cannot be executed if it cannot be understood, however, and it cannot be understood if it cannot be described. If we are going to create a Diversity and Inclusion (D&I) management process to implement an organizational and/or a D&I business strategy, we must first construct a reliable and consistent framework for describing the D&I strategy. No generally accepted framework existed, however, for describing information age strategies. D-BAMs help fill this void.

The financial framework worked well when competitive strategies were based on acquiring and managing tangible assets. In today's knowledge economy utilizing diverse human capital assets, sustainable value is created from developing intangible assets, such

D-BAM: Diversity Business Alignment Maps

as the skills and knowledge of the diverse workforce, the information technology that supports the diverse workforce and links the firm to its diverse customers and suppliers, and the organizational climate that encourages innovation, problem-solving, and improvement. Each of these intangible assets can contribute to value creation. But several factors prevent the financial measurements—used in traditional, industrial age, management control systems—from measuring these assets and linking them to value creation. Here is another example which demonstrates how creating value from intangible assets differs from creating value by managing tangible physical and financial assets:

1. Value Is Indirect. Intangible assets such as knowledge and technology seldom have a direct impact on the financial outcomes of revenue and profit. Improvements in intangible assets affect financial outcomes through chains of cause-and-effect relationships involving two or three intermediate stages. For example: Investments in employee training lead to improvements in service quality Better service quality leads to higher customer satisfaction Higher customer satisfaction leads to increased customer loyalty Increased customer loyalty generates increased revenues and margins The financial outcomes are separated causally and temporally from improving the intangible assets. The

D-BAM: Diversity Business Alignment Maps

complex linkages make it difficult if not impossible to place a financial value on an asset such as "workforce capabilities."

2. Value Is Contextual. The values of intangible assets depend on organizational context and strategy. They cannot be valued separately from the organizational processes that transform them into customer and financial outcomes. For example, a senior investment banker in a firm such as Goldman Sachs has immensely valuable capabilities for developing and managing customer relationships. That same person, with the same skills and experience, would be worth little to a company, such as E*TRADE.com, that emphasizes operational efficiency, low cost, and technology-based trading. The value of most intangible assets depends critically on the context—the organization, the strategy, the complementary assets—in which the intangible assets are deployed.

3. Value Is Potential. Tangible assets, such as raw material, land, and equipment, can be valued separately based on their historic cost—the traditional financial accounting method—or on various definitions of market value, such as replacement cost and realizable value. Industrial age companies succeeded by combining and transforming their tangible resources into products whose value exceeded their acquisition cost. Profit margins measured how much value was created beyond the costs required to acquire and transform tangible assets into finished products and services.

D-BAM: Diversity Business Alignment Maps

Companies today can measure the cost of developing their intangible assets—the training of employees, the spending on databases, the advertising to create brand awareness. But such costs are poor approximations of any realizable value created by investing in these intangible assets. Intangible assets have potential value but not market value until they are "**utilized**". Organizational processes, such as design, delivery, and service, are required to transform the potential value of intangible assets into products and services that have tangible value. That is why I am fond of stating that Diversity is not only about "representation". To have ROI-based value, Diversity and Inclusion must heavily focus on how diverse human capital assets are "utilized" (Not just counting heads, i.e., representation) but making sure that heads count through their "inclusion" and utilization.

4. **Assets Are Bundled.** Intangible assets seldom have value by themselves (brand names, which can be sold, are an exception). Generally, intangible assets must be bundled with other assets—intangible and tangible—to create value. For example, a new growth-oriented sales strategy could require new knowledge about customers, new training for sales employees, new databases, new information systems, a new organization structure, and a new incentive compensation program. Investing in just one of these capabilities, or in all of them but one, would cause the new sales strategy to fail.

D-BAM: Diversity Business Alignment Maps

The value does not reside in any individual intangible asset. It arises from creating the entire set of assets along with a strategy that links them together. The **Balanced Scorecard** and the **Diversity Scorecard** provide new frameworks to describe a strategy by linking intangible and tangible assets in value-creating activities. The scorecard does not attempt to "value" an organization's intangible assets. It does measure these assets, but in units other than currency (dollars, yen, and euros). In this way, the Balanced Scorecard can use strategy maps of cause-and-effect linkages to describe how intangible assets get mobilized and combined with other assets, both intangible and tangible, to create value -- creating customer value propositions and desired financial outcomes. Remember, a strategy map is a logical architecture that defines a strategy by specifying the relationships among shareholders, customers, business processes, and competencies. Strategy maps provide the foundation for building Balanced Scorecards linked to an organization's strategy. Strategy Maps play a *critical role* in addressing the adage: "*You can't manage it* (The Strategy-focused Organization component – reflected in an organization trying to achieve breakthrough results) *if you can't measure it* (the Balanced Scorecard component); *and you can't measure what you can't describe* (The Strategy component – reflected in the Strategy Map component).

D-BAM: Diversity Business Alignment Maps

A strategy map for a Balanced Scorecard makes explicit the strategy's hypotheses. Each measure of a Balanced Scorecard becomes embedded in a chain of cause-and-effect logic that connects the desired outcomes from the strategy with the drivers that will lead to the strategic outcomes. The strategy map describes the process for transforming intangible assets into tangible customer and financial outcomes. It provides executives with a framework for describing and managing strategy in a knowledge economy. A Balanced Scorecard strategy map is a generic architecture for describing a strategy. As an example, let's examine two diagrams. The first diagram illustrates the architecture of a strategy map for a retail firm specializing in women's clothing. The cause-and-effect logic of this design constitutes the hypotheses of the strategy. The financial perspective contains two themes—growth and productivity—for improving shareholder value. The value proposition in the customer perspective clearly emphasizes the importance of fashion, fit, and a complementary product line for the growth strategy. Four strategic themes in the internal perspective—brand dominance, fashion excellence, sourcing and distribution, and the shopping experience—deliver the value proposition to customers and drive the financial productivity theme.

D-BAM: Diversity Business Alignment Maps

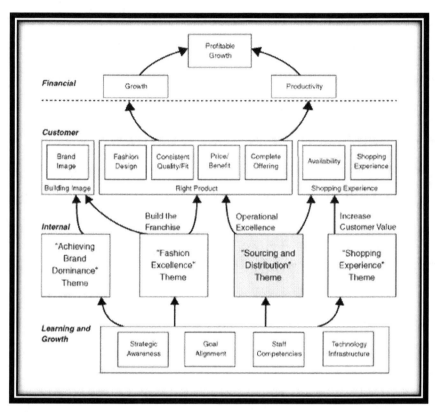

Kaplan, Robert S.; Norton, David P.. The Strategy-Focused Organization: How Balanced Scorecard Companies Thrive in the New Business Environment (Kindle Location 1247). Harvard Business Review Press. Kindle Edition.

The second diagram shows the detailed strategy map and Balanced Scorecard for one of the four strategic themes: sourcing and distribution. The diagram shows how this theme affects the customer objectives of product quality and product availability that, in turn, drive customer retention and revenue growth. Two internal processes—the factory management program and the line planning process—also contribute to these objectives. The former determines the quality of the factories used for manufacturing the

D-BAM: Diversity Business Alignment Maps

product, and the latter determines the quantities, mix, and location. New skills and information systems support both of these processes. The strategy map and scorecard for the sourcing and distribution theme define the logic of the approach to improving product, quality, and availability. The cause-and-effect relationships on the strategy map—and map—and the measures, targets, and initiatives on the scorecard—comprise the strategy for this theme.

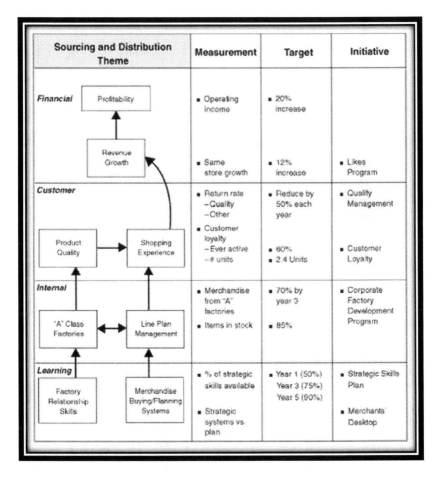

D-BAM: Diversity Business Alignment Maps

Strategy maps are important because they help organizations see their strategies in a cohesive, integrated, and systematic way. Executives often describe the outcome from constructing this mapping framework as "the best understanding of strategy we have ever had." And beyond just understanding, strategy maps provide the foundation for the management system for executing strategy effectively and rapidly. The Balanced Scorecard overcomes the limitations of purely financial measurement systems by clearly portraying the value-creating processes and critical roles for intangible assets.

The scorecard describes the multiple indirect linkages required to connect improvements in an organization's intangible assets—the ultimate drivers of knowledge-based strategies—to the tangible customer and financial outcomes from the strategy. The customer value proposition defines the context for how the diverse intangible assets create value. For example, if "fashion and design" are part of the customer value proposition, then an intangible asset, such as merchandising skill, is necessary for the strategy to succeed. If the "fashion and design" choices are part of an ethnic customer's value proposition, then intangible assets, such as multicultural merchandising and cultural competency skills may be required for the strategy to succeed.

The strategic themes describe the "recipe" for combining the intangible ingredients of skills, technologies, and organizational

D-BAM: Diversity Business Alignment Maps

climate with internal processes, such as sourcing and distribution, to create tangible outcomes—customer loyalty, revenue growth, and profitability. In this way, the Balanced Scorecard provides the measurement and management framework for knowledge-based strategies that are reflected in the strategy map.

Strategy Is a Step In a Continuum

Strategy does not (or should not) stand alone as a management process. A continuum exists that begins in the broadest sense, with the mission of the organization. The mission must be translated so that the actions of individuals are aligned and supportive of the mission. A management system should ensure that this translation is effectively made. Strategy is one step in a logical continuum that moves an organization from a high-level mission statement to the work performed by frontline and back-office employees. If we are to build a consistent architecture for describing strategy, we must have a consistent way of positioning it relative to other management processes. The figure below presents a view of strategy that helps to explain its ability to translate mission into desired outcomes. The overarching mission of the organization provides the starting point; it defines why the organization exists or how a business unit fits within a broader corporate architecture.

D-BAM: Diversity Business Alignment Maps

Translating Mission into Desired Outcomes

Kaplan, Robert S.; Norton, David P.. The Strategy-Focused Organization: How Balanced Scorecard Companies Thrive in the New Business Environment (Kindle Locations 1280-1285). Harvard Business Review Press. Kindle Edition.

The mission and the core values that accompany it remain fairly stable over time. The organization's vision paints a picture of the future that clarifies the direction of the organization and helps individuals to understand why and how they should support the organization. In addition, it launches the movement from the stability of the mission and core values to the dynamism of strategy, the next step in the continuum. Strategy is developed and

D-BAM: Diversity Business Alignment Maps

evolves over time to meet the changing conditions posed by the real world.

What are "Diversity Business Alignment Maps (D-BAM)?"

Like Balanced Scorecard Strategy Maps, Diversity Business Alignment Maps (D-BAMs) are also an architectural framework for describing how the Diversity and Inclusion Strategy is linked and aligned with the organization's Mission, Vision, Values and strategy. The D-BAM makes explicit how the Diversity Business Alignment Map will help drive core elements of the organization's business objectives, processes, intangible diverse human capital, the Diversity and Inclusion Strategic Plan and the Diversity Scorecard to create "value-added" outcomes for the organization.

Each measure of a Diversity Scorecard becomes embedded in a chain of cause-and-effect logic that connects the desired outcomes from the strategy with the drivers that will lead to the strategic outcomes. The Diversity Business Alignment Map drives the process for transforming diverse intangible asset capabilities into tangible customer and financial outcomes. It provides executives with a framework for describing, executing, and managing the Diversity and Inclusion strategy in a knowledge-based economy.

D-BAM: Diversity Business Alignment Maps

An example of a basic enterprise D-BAM is shown below:

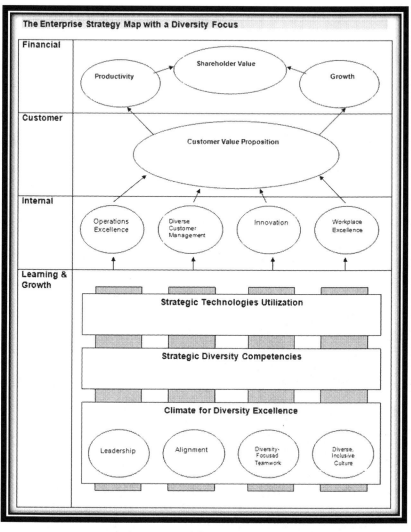

This diagram illustrates the sample architecture of a basic enterprise-wide strategy map. The cause-and-effect logic of this design constitutes the hypotheses of the strategy. The financial perspective contains two themes—growth and productivity—for

D-BAM: Diversity Business Alignment Maps

improving shareholder value. The value proposition in the customer perspective clearly emphasizes the importance of delivering measurable value for the productivity and growth strategies. Four strategic themes in the internal perspective—Operations Excellence, Diverse Customer Management, Innovation and Workplace Excellence drive the means to have impact on the two primary themes. The Operations Excellence and Diverse Customer Management processes allow the diversity organization to help drive the "Productivity" theme. The Innovation and Workplace Excellence processes allow the diversity organization to help drive the "Growth" theme.

The learning and growth perspective identifies the intangible assets that are most important to the strategy. The objectives in this perspective identify key leadership roles to ensure effective management and leadership throughout the organization, strengthen strategic alignment, build a diverse talented team, and integrate critical processes and behaviors to generate a diverse and inclusive culture.

It lays out a core framework to fully utilize additional intangible resources such as Strategic Technologies, Strategic Diversity Competencies reflected in the diverse human capital experiences that provide invaluable information and resource inputs to problems and opportunities.

D-BAM: Diversity Business Alignment Maps

This basic enterprise D-BAM can serve as a helpful template to begin mapping out your strategic approach to demonstrate the *"unique and sustainable ways by which the Diversity and Inclusion organization will create value for the organization"*. Templates, strategic themes, and intangible assets are the building blocks for understanding and executing strategy. They provide increased granularity for executives to describe and manage strategy at an operational level of detail.

Full Diversity Business Alignment Maps, such as the diagram shown below, build on these basic structures and principles and add complexity and customization to reflect the unique business goals, objectives and other requirements to achieve the future-state of the organization's strategic plan. These D-BAMs utilize an integrated, holistic approach to utilize Diversity and Inclusion strategies as performance improvement solution strategies to resolve challenging problems and opportunities in the organization's competitive marketplace. An example of one type of Hubbard & Hubbard, Inc. D-BAM is shown below:

D-BAM: Diversity Business Alignment Maps

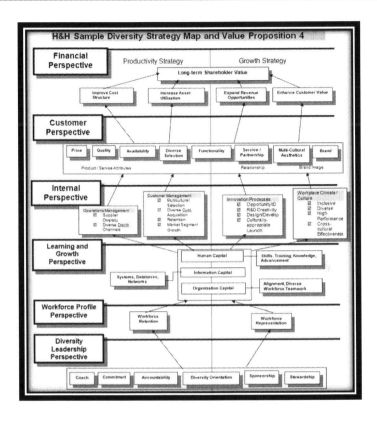

The importance of strategy to address real business issues using Diversity Business Alignment Maps cannot be underestimated or taken for granted. It is imperative that Diversity professionals become skilled and capable in their use and implementation. Most strategies – plans for producing specific business outcomes, fail to deliver their promised results. The problem usually doesn't lie in the strategy planning process; it lies in the execution process – the steps taken to carry out the strategic plan. Even the most brilliant strategy represented in the D-BAM is useless if people throughout the organization **cannot put the strategy into action**. Throughout

D-BAM: Diversity Business Alignment Maps

the rest of this book we will explore the remaining aspects of the D-BAM process and will cover steps you can take to ensure the strategy integrated into the D-BAM process delivers as promised.

So, let's get started!

References

Harvard Business School Press. Thinking Strategically (Pocket Mentor). Harvard Business Review Press. Pages 4-10.

Kaplan, Robert S.; Norton, David P.. The Strategy-Focused Organization: How Balanced Scorecard Companies Thrive in the New Business Environment (Kindle Locations 1177-1181). Harvard Business Review Press. Kindle Edition.

Kaplan, Robert S.; Norton, David P.. The Strategy-Focused Organization: How Balanced Scorecard Companies Thrive in the New Business Environment (Kindle Locations 1190-1195). Harvard Business Review Press. Kindle Edition.

Kaplan, Robert S.; Norton, David P.. Strategy Maps: Converting Intangible Assets into Tangible Outcomes (Kindle Locations 99-114). Harvard Business Review Press. Kindle Edition.

Kaplan, Robert S.; Norton, David P.. The Strategy-Focused Organization: How Balanced Scorecard Companies Thrive in the New Business Environment (Kindle Locations 1248-1253). Harvard Business Review Press. Kindle Edition.

Kaplan, Robert S.; Norton, David P.. The Strategy-Focused Organization: How Balanced Scorecard Companies Thrive in the New Business Environment (Kindle Locations 1266-1271). Harvard Business Review Press. Kindle Edition.

D-BAM: Diversity Business Alignment Maps

Kaplan, Robert S.; Norton, David P.. Strategy Maps: Converting Intangible Assets into Tangible Outcomes (Kindle Locations 3213-3220). Harvard Business Review Press. Kindle Edition.

Kaplan, Robert S.; Norton, David P.. Strategy Maps: Converting Intangible Assets into Tangible Outcomes (Kindle Locations 3220-3227). Harvard Business Review Press. Kindle Edition.

Hubbard, Edward E. *Measuring Diversity Results*. Petaluma, CA: Global Insights, 1997

Hubbard, Edward E. *How to Calculate Diversity Return on Investment*. Petaluma, CA: Global Insights, 1999.

Hubbard, Edward E. *The Diversity Scorecard*. Petaluma, CA: Elsevier Butterworth-Heinemann, 2004.

Hubbard, Edward E. *The Manager's Pocket Guide to Diversity Management*. Amherst, MA: HRD Press, 2003

Chapter Two: The Business Case for Diversity

A Diversity Measurement Challenge: How Can We Ensure that Diversity Is "at" the Strategic Business Table, Not "on" the Menu?

Many diversity professionals and others interested in diversity have asked the following questions:

- How will we be able to demonstrate that Diversity contributes to the organization's bottom line?
- How do we show senior executives and others that Diversity is a strategic business partner that is aligned and linked to the strategic goals and objectives of the organization?
- How can we measure the impact of Diversity on organizational performance and an improved work environment?
- How does the strategic Diversity process help an organization excel in the domestic and global marketplace and provide favorable returns to stockholders and stakeholders?

D-BAM: Diversity Business Alignment Maps

If your organization is like most, you have probably found it challenging to answer these questions. Experience has shown that the Diversity organization has its own brand of strategy and visions and has developed its own perspective regarding the value of its efforts to implement a diverse work environment; however, senior leaders and line management are skeptical, at best, of diversity's impact on the organization's success and their ability to demonstrate any financial or strategic contributions that a diverse workforce makes to the bottom line. In many firms, executives and others want to believe the cliché that views people as the organization's most important asset; however, they simply cannot understand how diversity realistically makes that vision a reality that results in a measurable difference in organizational performance.

Organizations typically define their Diversity efforts in terms of race and gender, which get reflected in the elements they track regularly. This list is usually sorted by demographic group and might include items such as number recruited, employee turnover, cost per hire, number of minority personnel or women on the organization's board of directors, and employee attitudes. Now consider those diversity attributes that push beyond race and gender that you believe are crucial to implementing your organization's competitive strategy. In this list, you might include items such as penetrating diverse customer markets, retaining

D-BAM: Diversity Business Alignment Maps

capable and committed diverse work teams that generate new, paradigm-shifting ideas in half the time of competitors, new patents that are generated through diverse teams working on innovative approaches, improving customer issue resolution processes, reducing cycle time, increasing market share and shareholder value, and the like.

How well do your existing processes illustrate the strategies you use to help drive the accomplishment of the organization's business objectives? How well do your existing diversity measures capture the strategic Diversity drivers you identified in the second list? For most organizations, there will not be a very close match between the two lists. Even more important, in those firms where diversity professionals think there is a close match, the senior executives frequently do not agree that this second list actually describes how Diversity creates value. In either case, a serious disconnect exists between what is measured and what is important to organizational performance. This highlights why constructing a Diversity Business Alignment Map (D-BAM) is essential to illustrate the connection to the organization's Vision, Mission, Values, and key business outcomes (see Sample Hubbard D-BAM with Diversity Strategy on the following page).

D-BAM: Diversity Business Alignment Maps

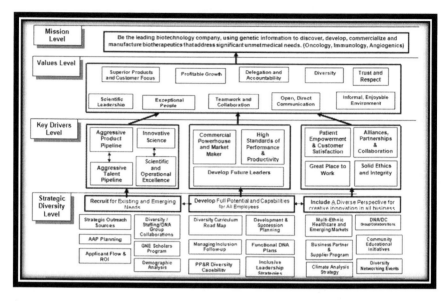

Sample Hubbard D-BAM with Diversity Strategy

These questions are fundamental because new economic realities are putting pressure on organizations to widen their traditional focus of Diversity as the guardian of ethnic representation and social well-being to a broader, more strategic factor in business success. As a primary source of production and performance impact, our economy has shifted from physical to intellectual capital (which comes in all colors, backgrounds, genders, orientations, thinking styles, and so on). As a result, senior Diversity managers are increasingly coming under fire to demonstrate exactly how they are helping the organization organize, utilize, and document this critically significant organizational asset to create performance and value.

D-BAM: Diversity Business Alignment Maps

The primary issue that Diversity must deal with is difficult for some to imagine and believe (i.e., showing diversity's measurable impact on organizational strategy and the financial bottom line). The ability to utilize a diverse mixture of human and other resources to create a unique blend of strategy-focused solutions, by its very nature, creates an innovative competitive process that is difficult to copy—thus making it a competitive advantage (largely invisible to competitors).

Simply put, utilizing Diversity as a strategic asset keeps an organization's competitive edge sharp for the long haul. This makes Diversity a prime source of sustainable competitive potential. To realize this potential, however, diversity professionals must understand the organization's strategic plan for developing and sustaining this competitive advantage throughout the organization and its marketplace. In order to gain its benefits, this Diversity must be utilized.

Can a Perceived Intangible Asset Like Diversity Generate Tangible Benefits?

Yes, it can! Executives and other organizational personnel are beginning to recognize the importance and benefits of calculating the impact of perceived intangible human assets in today's marketplace. This has been challenging in the past for a number of reasons. As Becker, Huselid, and Ulrich (2001) point out, the

D-BAM: Diversity Business Alignment Maps

accounting systems in use today evolved during a time when tangible capital, both financial and physical, constituted the principal source of profits. During this time, they state, those organizations that had the most access to money and equipment enjoyed a huge competitive advantage. With today's economic emphasis on knowledge and intangible assets, however, conventional accounting systems actually create dangerous informational distortions. As just one example, these systems encourage limited, short-term thinking with respect to managing intangibles. Why? Because expenditures in these areas are treated as expenses rather than investments in assets. In contrast to this view, investments in buildings and machinery are capitalized and depreciated over their useful lives.

Consider the following dilemma faced by executives and managers: Decide whether to invest $10 million in hard assets or $10 million in people. In practical terms, when an organization invests $10 million in a building or physical asset, this investment is depreciated over time and earnings are reduced gradually over a 20- to 30-year period. In contrast, a $10 million investment in people is expensed in its entirety (and therefore earnings are reduced by $10 million) during the current year. For executives and managers whose pay is tied to this year's earnings (as many are), the choice of which investment to make is clear.

D-BAM: Diversity Business Alignment Maps

As a result, organizations under financial pressure tend to invest in physical capital at the expense of human capital—even though the latter may very well generate more value. This kind of pressure can lead to poor decision-making behavior, such as using personnel layoffs, downsizing, and right-sizing to generate short-term cost savings. We know from past experience that after a layoff, the market may initially respond with a jump in share value; however, investors often eventually lose most, if not all, of these gains. This pattern is not surprising, given that people are a crucial source of competitive advantage rather than an expensive luxury that should be minimized.

The clear bottom line is this: If current accounting methods cannot give Diversity professionals the measurement tools they need, then it is imperative that we, as Diversity professionals, develop our own ways of demonstrating Diversity's contribution to the organization's performance. Like any other discipline, Diversity must be composed of both solid theory and applied sciences to gain credibility as a key contributor to organizational performance. At some point, the theory has to be put into practice and evaluated for its ability to add measurable value and understanding to real organizational issues.

We have evidence of a great deal of solid Diversity theory, such as those put forth by R. Roosevelt Thomas (1991,1996, 1999), Judith Rosner (1991), Marilyn Loden (1996), Taylor Cox (1993, 1997),

D-BAM: Diversity Business Alignment Maps

and many others; however, notwithstanding the seminal Diversity measurement work completed by Edward E. Hubbard (1997, 1999), 2004, 20010, et.al., the Hubbard Diversity Measurement and Productivity Institute's research, and a chapter on the subject by Lawrence M. Baytos (1995), there has been little scientific inquiry research and operational processes that measure the real financial impact of Diversity.

The first step in building a diversity contribution process is to discard the accounting mentality that suggests diversity or human resource–based efforts are primarily cost centers in which cost minimization is the primary objective and measure of success. At the same time, it is important to take advantage of the opportunity to help define the standards for measuring diversity's impact. Investors and organizations such as the Swedish firm Skandia have made it clear that intangible assets are important. Skandia, for example, includes intellectual assets as a normal part of its profit and loss (P&L) reporting.

Dr. Edward E. Hubbard pioneered efforts to create a wide variety of measures for the Diversity field in his books *Measuring Diversity Results* (1997), *How to Calculate Diversity Return on Investment* (1999), *The Diversity Scorecard: Evaluating the Impact of Diversity on Organizational Performance* (2004), *Implementing Diversity Measurement and Diversity Management* (2004), *Diversity Training ROI* (2010), *Measuring the ROI Impact of*

D-BAM: Diversity Business Alignment Maps

ERGs and BRGs (2014), *Diversity Return On Investment (DROI) Fundamentals* (2014), and many more. He has written over 40 Diversity Measurement and Business-related books and hundreds of articles on the subject. In addition to these books, Dr. Hubbard founded the Hubbard Diversity Measurement and Productivity (HDM&P) Institute. The HDM&P Institute is dedicated to creating applied sciences for measuring diversity performance and results to improve organizational performance. It is really up to diversity professionals to develop a new measurement system that creates real value for the organization. This will help position the Diversity and Inclusion organization as a legitimate strategic business partner.

A key ingredient of any organization's success is its ability to strategically utilize human capital and leverage performance-based measurement feedback as a competitive advantage. To sustain success, maintain high productivity levels, retain talented employees, create new systems, and keep its diverse customer base, an organization must know its strengths and weaknesses in order to improve its overall performance. It is critical to have the diversity tools and systems required to lead a measurement-managed diversity implementation strategy. These tools must channel the energies, abilities, and specific knowledge held by a diverse workforce throughout the organization toward achieving its long-term strategic goals and objectives.

D-BAM: Diversity Business Alignment Maps

Diversity Facts, Figures, and Financial Performance

Diversity professionals are increasingly challenged to take a more strategic perspective regarding their role in producing results for the organization. As Diversity professionals respond to these challenges, measuring the impact of Diversity and its contribution to the organization's performance will consistently emerge as a critical theme. This should really come as no surprise because over the last 5 to 7 years there has been an ever-increasing appreciation for the value of the softer people side or intangible assets of the organization's business and an associated trend toward strategic performance measurement systems, such as those of Robert Kaplan and David Norton's *The Balanced Scorecard* (1996). The D-BAM process provides a strategic, systemic approach to operationalize the Diversity strategy as an "integrated" methodology to reap the benefits of utilizing Diversity and Inclusion as a measurable performance improvement technology. This approach provides a strategy to address business challenges head on.

During the past few years, several surveys of executives and human resource professionals have identified broad areas of Diversity as one of the top priorities now and in the immediate future. Certainly, the growth of consulting firms, seminars, conferences, and publications are evidence of the interest and

D-BAM: Diversity Business Alignment Maps

needs of organizations. The staying power of diversity as a corporate priority has been demonstrated by the high level of interest that carried through even the recession periods of the 90s and the beginning of the 21st century. In fact, in our past during the early part of the 90s, Towers Perrin reported in a survey that 96 percent of the responding companies had either maintained or increased their support for diversity management during the recession. The HDM&P Institute conducted a diversity measurement benchmarking survey in 2001 that reflected similar results. This survey found that 83 percent of the responding organizations planned to spend either the same amount or more on Diversity in 2002. Studies by organizations such as the Association for Talent Development (ATD – formerly ASTD) and i4cp) highlight the continued interest in Diversity. Yet at the same time, current studies indicate that the C-Suite has requested Diversity and Inclusion demonstrate measurable returns on the organization's investments in these areas and are sadly disappointed with the reporting and the results. The D-BAM Methodology and model overcomes these weaknesses and helps deliver real measurable value to C-Suite to meet Stakeholder requirements. The business case for Diversity is compelling and must be addressed using critical business acumen and scientific processes to level-set Diversity and Inclusion as a strategic business partner like other areas of the business.

D-BAM: Diversity Business Alignment Maps

What Do We Mean by Diversity?

To begin, what do we mean by the term *"Diversity"*? According to Dr. R. Roosevelt Thomas, *"Diversity* can be defined as a collective mixture characterized by differences and similarities that are applied in pursuit of organizational objectives" (Thomas, 1996, 1999). *Diversity management* is "the process of planning for, organizing, directing, and supporting these collective mixtures in a way that adds a measurable difference to organizational performance." (Hubbard, 1999)

Diversity management, according to Dr. Hubbard, can be organized into four interdependent and sometimes overlapping aspects: Workforce Diversity, Behavioral Diversity, Structural Diversity, and Business and Global Diversity (Hubbard, 1999).

Workforce Diversity encompasses group and situational identities of the organization's employees (i.e., gender, race, ethnicity, religion, sexual orientation, physical ability, age, family status, economic background and status, and geographical background and status). It also includes changes in the labor market demographics.

Behavioral Diversity encompasses work styles, thinking styles, learning styles, communication styles, aspirations, beliefs/value system, as well as changes in employees' attitudes and expectations.

D-BAM: Diversity Business Alignment Maps

Structural Diversity encompasses interactions across functions, across organizational levels in the hierarchy, across divisions and between parent companies and subsidiaries, and across organizations engaged in strategic alliances and cooperative ventures. As organizations attempt to become more flexible, less layered, more team-based, and more multi- and cross-functional, measuring this type of diversity will require more attention.

Business and Global Diversity encompasses the expansion and segmentation of customer markets, the diversification of products and services offered, and the variety of operating environments in which organizations work and compete (i.e., legal and regulatory context, labor market realities, community and societal expectations/relationships, business cultures and norms). Increasing competitive pressures, globalization, rapid advances in product technologies, changing demographics in the customer bases both within domestic markets and across borders, and shifts in business/government relationships all signal a need to measure an organization's response and impact on business Diversity.

Lawrence Bayos (1995) suggested that the 3 Ds have generated widespread corporate concern and interest in addressing diversity management issues, whether an organization has 100 or 100,000 employees. The 3 Ds are as follows:

D-BAM: Diversity Business Alignment Maps

Demographics. Females, minorities, and foreign-born personnel are projected to produce 85 percent of the net new growth in the U.S. workforce, while white males are fast becoming a minority in the workforce. In 1960, nine out of ten consumers were white. Currently, it is estimated that only six out of ten are white. The changing demographics of the workplace are also the changing demographics of the marketplace. Organizations are looking at ways to align their organizations to the new realities of their customer bases.

Disappointment. The traditional U.S. method for handling diversity was to bring women and people of color into the workforce under the banner of affirmative action. In doing so, it is often assumed that those individuals possess some deficiencies and may not have been hired if not for affirmative action. It was also assumed that they should be willing to assimilate their differences to better fit the norms of the majority group (usually white males) and thereby enhance their opportunities for recognition and advancement. In other words, to "make it," females and people of color would have to leave their needs and differences at the organization's front door. After a little more than three decades of affirmative action, it seems clear that the existing model has resulted in females and people of color being trapped in lower levels of the organizational pyramid. Turnover, discontent, and

D-BAM: Diversity Business Alignment Maps

underutilization of talent are by-products of using the previous approaches for several decades.

Demands. The demands for new approaches to Diversity come from employees who have become less willing than their predecessors to assimilate their points of difference in hopes of gaining the elusive acceptance into the club. Furthermore, the intense pressure of industry and global competition to reengineer the organization requires that organizations tap the full potential of all their human assets.

Diversity Provides a Business Advantage

Organizations that want to thrive in today's global marketplace know that they have to focus well beyond adding technology, efficient production processes, and innovative products. In fact, it can be argued that none of these approaches will add significantly measurable improvements unless all employees have an environment that allows them to do their absolute personal best work using their full capability. Forward-thinking organizations know that their competitive strength lies in focusing on their employees and their clients. For an organization to improve performance and results, it must be able to attract, motivate, and retain high-potential employees—including men and women from all backgrounds and walks of life.

D-BAM: Diversity Business Alignment Maps

In addition to attracting and retaining the best workforce, successful businesses must also attract and retain clients. The ability to retain clients can have a major impact on the organization's bottom line. For example, the lifetime revenue stream from a loyal pizza eater can be $12,000, a Cadillac owner $332,000, and a corporate purchaser of commercial aircraft literally billions of dollars (Haskett et al., 1994). A White House Office of Consumer Affairs study estimates that 90 percent of unhappy customers will not tell you they are unhappy with your service. Only 10 percent will complain. They also estimate that each unhappy person will tell nine other people about your poor service. They in turn will tell nine others. Therefore, 81 people will learn about your poor service.

If your business is a local coffee shop and 100 diverse customers (who order a $3 Café Mocha each week) were unhappy with your service, these potential $3–per-week coffee-drinking customers can potentially affect the success of your business in a major way, which may not be completely obvious until it is too late. For example, if these 100 unhappy customers tell nine others, 900 people will know about your poor service. If they choose not to come to your coffee shop for one day per week, then you have just potentially lost $1,263,600 in one year from only 100 customers!

Globalization and changing domestic markets reflect a changing buying public. It is no longer homogeneous. There is little doubt

D-BAM: Diversity Business Alignment Maps

that an organization that is serious about diversity can gain an improved understanding of diverse customers' needs and therefore foster better customer service to an increasingly diverse market.

Some of the latest American workforce projections put forth by the U.S. Department of Labor indicate that only 15 percent of the new entrants to the workforce will be white males and nearly 85 percent will be women, minorities, and immigrants. "In 50 of America's 200 cities with populations over 100,000, the so-called minority is the majority. Workers 55 and older are the fastest growing segment of the workforce. By some estimates, one in 10 Americans is gay. And technology is enabling more and more people with disabilities to enter the workforce".

The global marketplace has opened up a wide range of possibilities for organizational performance and success. Many organizations are broadening their potential markets beyond U.S. borders to include China, India, the Pacific Rim, all parts of Europe, South Africa, and the like. These organizations realize that differences in language, culture, processes, and business practices must be acknowledged to successfully enter these markets. In addition, they must learn from these diverse experiences and incorporate the skills, beliefs, and/or practices into organizational processes to capitalize on diversity for a competitive advantage.

D-BAM: Diversity Business Alignment Maps

One study by Poole highlights the following example: An American investment bank experienced problems when it launched an aggressive expansion plan into Europe. Their relocated American employees lacked credibility, were ignorant of local cultural norms and market conditions, and could not connect with their new clients. The investment bank responded to this problem by hiring Europeans who had attended North American business schools and assigning them in teams to the foreign offices. This strategy was enormously successful. The European operations were highly profitable and were staffed by a truly international group of professionals; however, the investment bank realized it still had a problem. If the French team, the German team, or the team in another country suddenly resigned, they would be right back where they were 10 years ago. The investment bank had not learned what the cultural differences really were or how they change the process of doing business. Cultural identity issues were never talked about openly. While they knew enough to use people's cultural strengths, they never internalized them or learned from them. Differences were valued, but they were not valued enough to be integrated into the organization's culture and business practices. In order to implement an effective diversity process, the investment bank needed to incorporate the extra steps to ensure that diversity was fully integrated into the organization's culture, skill sets, and functioning as a strategic capability issue.

D-BAM: Diversity Business Alignment Maps

Events such as mergers and acquisitions, changing customer marketplace demographics, and the like require organizations to work together. Organizations are also realizing that system flexibility, teamwork, measurement, and analysis is central to the drive for Six Sigma–level quality and innovation in products and services. Years of research have shown that well-managed, heterogeneous (diverse) groups will generally outperform homogeneous ones in problem solving, innovation, and creative solution building—exactly the capabilities that are critical to business success.

Organizations will have to be diverse because their customers are becoming more diverse, both abroad and in the United States. In the United States today, African Americans, Hispanics, Asian Americans, and Native Americans have an estimated combined spending power of more than $1.5 trillion. The shift to a service economy only increases the value of diverse employees, who may be better able to read and negotiate with such customers. The summary data below from the Selig Center for Economic Growth, Terry College of Business – The University of Georgia shows the spending power of minorities in the United States.

- **African-American buying power**, estimated at $1.2 trillion in 2016, will grow to $1.5 trillion by 2021, making it the largest racial minority consumer market. African-Americans constitute the nation's largest racial

D-BAM: Diversity Business Alignment Maps

minority market; however, the buying power of Hispanics (an ethnic minority group) is larger. Black buying power increased 98 percent from 2000 to 2016 and will comprise 8.8 percent of the nation's total buying power in 2021, according to the Selig Center.

- **Asian buying power** in 2014 was $770 billion and will rise to $1 trillion by 2019. Asian-Americans make up 6 percent of the population and control 6 percent of its purchasing power. Since 2000, Asian buying power has grown 222 percent to $891 billion, the biggest percentage increase of any U.S. minority group. U.S. Asian buying power exceeds the entire economies of all but 15 countries in the world. "The fast-paced growth of Asian consumers should create opportunities for businesses that pay attention to their needs and step in to serve niche markets,"

- **Hispanic buying power.** From a buying power estimate of $495 billion in 2000, the Hispanic group has increased its economic clout 181 percent to $1.4 trillion in 2016. That accounts for nearly 10 percent of total U.S. buying power in 2016 and means the U.S. Hispanic market is larger than the GDP of Mexico and bigger than the economies of all but 14 countries in the world.

- **Buying power of Native Americans** in 2014 was $100 billion, a 149 percent increase from 2000. The main

D-BAM: Diversity Business Alignment Maps

reason for the increase in buying power for Native American's is an increase in population. For example, from 2000 through 2014, the Native American population grew by 48.9 percent.

Source: Publication - The Multicultural Economy 2017, Minority spending power in the U.S., Selig Center for Economic Growth, University of Georgia, Terry College of Business).

African-Americans constitute the nation's largest racial minority market; however, the buying power of Hispanics (an ethnic minority group) is larger. Black buying power increased 98 percent from 2000 to 2016 and will comprise 8.8 percent of the nation's total buying power in 2021, according to the Selig Center.

Failure to Implement a Diversity Initiative Can Be Costly

If the lures of increased productivity, global marketing effectiveness, improved problem-solving performance, and enhanced creativity are not enough to initiate change in your organization's culture, the downside risks and impacts of turnover costs, poor training return-on-investment due to short tenure, poor overall brand image, failing community image as a good place to work for all employees, litigation charges, and the like is certainly worth considering. It can cost as much as $112,000 to recruit and train a full-time sales employee with a salary of $100,000 per year.

D-BAM: Diversity Business Alignment Maps

Other examples of retention costs include the following (Workplace News)

- $116,340 for a chief engineer with 17 years of service, earning $77,560 annually
- $110,000 for a government services underwriter with 11 years of service, earning $110,000 annually
- $105,000 for a vice president for 15 years of service, earning $63,000 annually
- $104,000 for a middle manager with 38 years of service, earning $52,000 annually
- $52,065 for a store manager with 21 years of service, earning $34,710 annually
- $44,888 for a shift foreperson with 14 years of service, earning $51,300 annually

In addition to these costs, there are lost productivity costs and dissatisfied client costs. Time, effort, and money must be spent on recruitment and selection to replace the employee who is leaving the organization. Lost productivity will result from the downtime created by the person leaving and the new employee's training and learning curve. Employees who are leaving, particularly those who believe they have not been treated fairly, are not likely to be overly productive after they hand in their resignations. New employees have to learn the job, the organizational structure, the formal rules, the informal rules, the workplace culture, and so on. This takes

D-BAM: Diversity Business Alignment Maps

time. These downtimes could even result in an organization's product or service being delivered late—resulting in extremely dissatisfied customers.

Typically, replacement costs are at least 1.5 times the yearly salary of employees. Replacement costs for women and people of color are higher because the time-to-fill rate can be longer if the organization has poor candidate source pools. These costs do not account for lost accumulated company knowledge or low morale where turnover is high. Add to this a whole host of legislation (e.g., Family and Medical Leave Act, Americans with Disabilities Act, Age Discrimination in Employment Act, Immigration Reform and Control Act of 1986), the cost of litigation with judgments exceeding $1- 4 million, and the price of rebuilding a corporate image because of negative publicity, and some of the economic reasons for retaining employees become clear.

Diversity Links to Productivity and Performance

It is no secret that employees who are treated with respect and integrity and who are given an opportunity to have input into their work, on average, perform at higher levels. Employees figure out the level of effort they are required to put into their work. There is little doubt that satisfied employees are going to be better workers (i.e., their productivity will be higher than that of unsatisfied employees). In addition, fair employment practices allow

D-BAM: Diversity Business Alignment Maps

organizations to more effectively attract, motivate, and retain the most qualified talent. Expectancy theory shows that treating employees fairly leads to higher levels of employee satisfaction and morale. An organization that has satisfied employees will find that it has low employee voluntary turnover (better known from an asset point of view as human capital depletion) and a highly productive workforce.

Research bears out the observation that employees who truly like their jobs and the organizations they work for tend to stay with the organization and have a positive impact on customer service and performance. One such body of research is the Service-Profit Chain developed by Haskett, Jones, Loveman, Sasser, and Schlesinger (1994). They established a causal pathway relationship that demonstrated that factors such as improving an organization's environment and an employee's satisfaction had a direct impact on customer satisfaction, retention, and loyalty, which generated a corresponding increase in organizational revenues and profits. In further research, Rucci, Quinn, and Kirn (1998) applied this Service-Profit Chain approach to organizational issues at Sears, Inc. and found that for every 5 percentage point improvement made in employee satisfaction, a 1.3 percentage point improvement in customer satisfaction and loyalty resulted, which drove a .5 percentage point improvement in store revenues. In one year, this accounted for an additional $200 million in revenue.

D-BAM: Diversity Business Alignment Maps

Employee satisfaction has a tremendous influence on employee commitment, which is reflected in key performance variables such as retention and productivity.

Retention

Employees will often cast their vote of dissatisfaction and level of commitment by using the "Law of Two Feet" (i.e., they go somewhere else). When this happens, it is usually already too late to recapture their commitment. Employees who are leaving, particularly those who believe they have not been treated fairly, are not likely to be overly productive after they hand in their resignations.

It has been estimated that when an exempt (salaried) employee leaves an organization, it costs the organization 1.5 times the salary of the person who must be replaced. At the nonexempt (hourly) level, the impact is equivalent to 6 months of salary and benefits. It should also be noted that these figures only represent the costs needed to get a new person in the door! Costs incurred—such as learning curve costs, acculturation costs, formal and informal rules coaching, building customer and co-worker relationships, and network building costs equal to at least 90 percent of the departing employee—can represent a tremendous drain on the bottom line. These downtimes could even result in an organization's products and services being late—resulting in dissatisfied customers. This

D-BAM: Diversity Business Alignment Maps

merely points out that it is critical that an organization manages employee retention and tracks who is leaving, for what reason, and at what cost.

When highly productive employees leave the organization, it can be disastrous. In many cases, high-performing employees are not allowed to work to their full potential because the workplace environment does not take employee differences and similarities into consideration as a competitive advantage. Dissatisfied employees will begin to look for work elsewhere. Under intense competition for the most qualified talent, an organization's ability to attract and retain high-caliber talent will depend in part on its reputation as an employer and whether employees are allowed to do their absolute personal best work. The consulting firm Deloitte & Touche, for example, found that it attracted more prospective employees after implementing Diversity initiatives. Both men and women stated that they wanted to work for a firm that is progressive and growing.

Conversely, a study conducted at a different workplace noted that women who do manage to get through the glass ceiling "feel so unsatisfied and undervalued that they leave early—and in proportionately greater numbers than their male counterparts." A study of 500 organizations found that nearly 40 percent of private-sector workers regularly think about quitting their jobs (Davis, 1996). Another workforce study showed that dissatisfied

D-BAM: Diversity Business Alignment Maps

employees were three times more likely than satisfied employees to indicate their intent to leave the organization (Haskett et al., 1994). When these things occur, organizations jeopardize their ability to meet strategic business objectives.

Productivity

Another result of poor employee satisfaction is its impact on productivity. Drew Davis noted in a study of 500 organizations that downsized because they thought downsizing would reduce costs, increase productivity, and encourage people to work smarter, that these organizations experienced varying results. The fear of downsizing, eroding trust, disillusionment, and frustration about dwindling promotion opportunities and job security caused employees to be demotivated and bitter. This had a devastating hidden effect on the organization's bottom line. Seventy-five percent of the 500 organizations found that employee morale had collapsed, and two-thirds of these organizations showed no increase in efficiency.

Productivity relates not only to direct effort but also to discretionary effort. This relates to the extra effort that employees give to their work. In today's workplaces, discretionary effort can make the difference between getting and not getting a client and between keeping and losing a client. Many organizations can replicate their competitors' technology, but they cannot replicate

D-BAM: Diversity Business Alignment Maps

their workforces. In an information- and intellectual capital–based society, competitive organizational capability will come through people—people who are valued regardless of their backgrounds and who are given the opportunity to be innovative and fully productive. Demotivated, non-valued employees will rarely expend the extra effort that may be required to win over customers and gain a competitive advantage.

Diverse work teams have been found to possess the potential to achieve higher levels of performance than homogeneous teams. Diverse groups of people bring a broad range of skills, knowledge, abilities, and perspectives to organizational challenges. Research has shown that diverse teams frequently develop more ideas and potential solutions to problems than homogeneous teams. Capowski described studies of four organizations: AT&T, Harris Bank, Northrup Grumman, and GE Power Systems. They found that the performance of the diverse work teams generated more ideas that evolved into new products and services than the performance of homogeneous teams. The latter group does not have as many perspectives to bring to the table as a diverse work team. The synergy that can be created by a homogeneous group of people is limited because they are so similar. With the proper training, diverse work teams can make the most of their varied perspectives and outperform homogeneous teams; however, homogeneous teams do come to the table with a common frame of

D-BAM: Diversity Business Alignment Maps

reference, and they know how to communicate effectively with each other.

Members of a diverse team are unlikely to have that knowledge and often must be trained in specific processes and techniques that effectively utilize their varied perspectives. To ensure effectiveness, team members must understand their differences, the communication process, group dynamics, and ways to integrate their many ideas into cohesive solutions. Diversity can "breed tension, conflict, misunderstandings, and frustration unless an organization develops a culture that supports, honors, and values differences" (Van Eron).

In the following examples, Addison Reid illustrates the impact of diversity on the bottom line of two organizations:

Example One. A Spanish speaker in the decision-making loop could have saved General Motors the expense of trying to market the Chevy Nova in Mexico. Nova is Spanish for "it doesn't go."

Example Two. If Gerber baby foods had known the local customs, it would have been saved the expense of recalling and relabeling jars and apologizing to its clients in one African country for suggesting that they were cannibals (nobody feed ground-up babies in a jar to other babies as the label implied!). In that country, it is customary for a label to picture the product, not the intended client.

D-BAM: Diversity Business Alignment Maps

Gerber, in its attempt to address Diversity, had simply changed the white baby on the label of their baby food jars to a black baby.

In both cases, this lack of Diversity awareness and diversity utilization cost the organizations millions of dollars in lost revenue and damage to its brand image—not to mention its major impact on productivity costs.

The Link Between the Lack of Diversity Programs and Absenteeism

Productivity is directly affected by the cost of absenteeism and hostile work environments. Satisfied employees are absent less often than unsatisfied employees, are late less often, are less apt to leave early, and are less apt to use expensive short-term and long-term disability benefits. Employees witnessing and/or experiencing hostile work environments and harassment are often away more often and are less productive. Imperial Oil of Canada estimates that harassment costs them close to $8 million annually in absenteeism, employee turnover, and loss of productivity. This does not include legal fees (Poole). This is a high price to pay for something that can be prevented.

If employees are staying with the organization and working well, customers are more apt to be happy and satisfied. While employee turnover costs money and time for recruiting, hiring, and training replacements, it also affects customer satisfaction. The employee

D-BAM: Diversity Business Alignment Maps

who left, for example, may have been in contact with the organization's customers, and the customers will now have to deal with someone new who does not understand their needs. The customer, more than likely, may have been satisfied with the employee who just left. This employee may have been their primary contact with the organization for the past five or so years. He or she knew the customer's special needs. Now the customer will have to deal with the new employee or choose to go somewhere else. An even more frightening scenario is that the customers follow the employee who is leaving your organization (who knows all of the company's secrets) to your competitor, taking their business with them.

One study showed that low employee turnover was found to be linked closely to high customer satisfaction. The study found that when an employee who had direct contact with a customer left, their customer satisfaction level dropped sharply from 75 percent to 55 percent (Haskett et al., 1994). Another study by Abt Associates concluded that there was an average monthly cost of $36,000 in sales for replacing a sales representative with five to eight years of experience with an employee who had less than one year of experience. Conservative estimates of replacing a broker at a securities firm concluded that it takes nearly five years for a broker to rebuild relationships with customers that can return $1 million per year in commissions to the brokerage house, which

D-BAM: Diversity Business Alignment Maps

amounts to a cumulative loss of at least $2.5 million in commission (Haskett et al., 1994).

Customers who know that their needs are going to be met are usually satisfied customers; however, as Janet Lapp (1996) points out, cynicism has developed among customers about what to expect from organizations. Many customers have low expectations about the ability of organizations to do what they say they will do or to be different from their competitors in a meaningful way. In order to be successful, organizations should be looking for ways to build strong, solid reputations for delivery and working to sustain the loyalty of their customers. Lapp points out that the "CEO of Starbucks believes that the quality of his workforce is the company's only sustainable, competitive advantage. He believes that workers need to feel pride in and to have a stake in the outcome of their efforts on the job." In essence, they must feel valued and included in the work climate and the decisions that affect their lives.

Diversity's Contribution to the Bottom Line

Satisfied customers tend to be loyal customers; not many satisfied customers go to the competition. One way of ensuring that customers are satisfied is to have a workforce that clearly reflects the organization's marketplace. This has become clear in the banking industry. Most banks, for example, offer about the same

D-BAM: Diversity Business Alignment Maps

rates; it is the people who make the difference—the customer service difference (Martinez, 1995). We know from past experience that satisfied and loyal customers often become lifelong customers bringing repeat business. Not only will this repeat business boost revenues, but satisfied and loyal customers will also make referrals. Referrals are one of the best ways to increase an organization's customer base and, in turn, its profitability. This includes direct referrals as well as pass-along referrals, where the customer brags about your organization and customers show up without any intervention (e.g., marketing, sales efforts) on your part. Satisfied customers also make excellent references when your business calls for them in a bidding situation. Good references can make the difference between being an unsuccessful bidder and winning the contract! Conversely, a dissatisfied customer can severely damage your organization's reputation and can affect future sales and profits.

In general, whenever an organization experiences customer-base growth, it translates into a better bottom line, increasing sales and profits. One study by Reicheld and Sasser (1990) found that a 5 percent increase in customer loyalty can produce profit increases that range from 25 to 85 percent. Organizations can determine customer loyalty by tracking customer retention, the number of services used by each customer, and the level of customer satisfaction. The strategies derived from this information helped

D-BAM: Diversity Business Alignment Maps

explain why one of the organizations studied had achieved a return on assets in recent years more than double that of its competitors (Haskett et al., 1994).

Organizations that have included diversity in their organizational goals realize the importance of investing in their employees and servicing the varying needs of their customers. Increases in profits give organizations an opportunity to spend more time and money to make certain the workplace meets the needs of all workers while providing a fair return to shareholders.

Organizations that do not have an effective Diversity process or no process at all will also incur costs, including high turnover, low morale, ineffective products or services, unproductive teams, inability to attract and retain employees, and legal and other expenses. Some well-known discrimination and bias cases from the past that illustrate this impact on the bottom line, however, in many ways, we still have not fully learned the lesson they generated and seem destined to repeat them. These cases included the following:

- Coca-Cola ($192.5M) Race
- State Farm ($250M) Gender
- Home Depot ($110M) Gender
- Lucky Stores ($107M) Gender
- Publix ($82M) Gender

D-BAM: Diversity Business Alignment Maps

- Texaco ($176M) Race
- Shoneys ($132M) Race
- Denny's ($54M) Race

Poorly implemented Diversity processes can damage an organization's reputation with current and future (potential) employees as well as current and future customers and investors. An effective process, on the other hand, will increase the organization's goodwill and reputation (Poole). By effectively measuring and tracking the costs and benefits of diversity, organizations truly understand that Diversity is a bottom-line business issue that is critical to organizational performance and results.

Building Centers of Diversity Excellence

Conducting diversity work as a strategic partner is some of the most important work we can do. It is critical to the myriad of customers served and vital to the people utilized inside the organization that diversity supports. Learning to serve as a strategic partner within the organizational structure is not just a way for Diversity practitioners to justify their existence or defend their turf. It has implications for the very survival of the diversity department and of the organization as a whole. If the Diversity function cannot show that it adds value, it risks being on the table for reduction, or worse—dismantling. With the right diversity

D-BAM: Diversity Business Alignment Maps

mindset and measurement tools, implementing diversity-strategic business objectives can mean the critical difference between an organization that is just keeping pace with the competition or one that is making major strides ahead. In essence, it requires creating centers of Diversity excellence using behavioral and technical ROI measurement capability, demonstrating commitment, and building communities of practice to sustain it over time.

In order for an organization to take full advantage of the potential wealth in its Diversity mixtures, it must completely embrace the level of Diversity required to meet critical organizational challenges head on. This occurs when organizations foster a climate and culture that values differences and maximizes the potential of employees through utilization—in other words, when the organization and the individuals within it operate in a mature fashion.

According to Dr. R. Roosevelt Thomas (1999), Diversity-maturity requires both an individual and organizational set of behaviors that drive success. He states that Diversity-mature individuals do the following:

- Accept personal responsibility for enhancing their own and their organization's effectiveness.

D-BAM: Diversity Business Alignment Maps

- Demonstrates contextual knowledge (i.e., they know themselves and their organizations and they understand key diversity concepts and definitions).
- Are clear about requirements and base include/exclude decisions about differences on how they impact the ability to meet these requirements.
- Understand that Diversity is accompanied by complexity and tension and are prepared to cope with these in pursuit of greater Diversity effectiveness.
- Are willing to challenge conventional wisdom.
- Engage in continuous learning.

Diversity-mature individuals see themselves, not others, as responsible for addressing Diversity effectively. They understand the impact of organizational culture on Diversity-related practices, but they do not use it as an excuse for inaction and indifference. Thomas points out that individuals aiming for greater Diversity effectiveness would do well to ask themselves the following personal Diversity questions:

- Am I comfortable working with people from all demographic groups?
- Is there a group or groups that I struggle to accept? If so, how have I attempted to overcome my biases?

D-BAM: Diversity Business Alignment Maps

- How will my comfort or lack of comfort with people different from me affect my ability to advance within this workplace?
- Do I enjoy Diversity? If so, what kind? If so, how much?

Diversity professionals are not exempt from these issues and must answer these questions for themselves. Diversity-mature individuals know that when people with different backgrounds, perspectives, and objectives express themselves openly, there will be tension. This tension is not inherently positive or negative, good or bad; it simply is. Tension that promotes healthy competition can be good. Tension that immobilizes a unit is clearly not. The difficulty is that many individuals, like organizations, are so uncomfortable with tension that they focus on eliminating it rather than managing it. They place more importance on harmony than on achieving objectives.

Diversity-mature individuals learn to function in the face of tension. They know it is not personal but rather part and parcel of the dynamics of diversity. Tension and conflict are not the same. Tension becomes conflict when it is responded to ineptly. Diversity conflict arises when people ask unproductive questions, such as, "What's wrong with you that you aren't more like me?" (Thomas, 1999). Diversity-mature individuals have challenged conventional wisdom and made mindset changes along the way that equip them to respond effectively to these challenges.

D-BAM: Diversity Business Alignment Maps

By adjusting to this new mindset and accepting personal responsibility for action, diversity practitioners can develop new competencies to fulfill their strategic roles. The new economic paradigm of diversity as a financial contributor requires diversity professionals to do different things and help the organization deal with the dynamic tension that comes with managing a diverse workforce. This means more than just understanding the organization's articulated strategy; it means that Diversity professionals must become strategic business partners who comprehend exactly what capabilities, environments, and other factors are needed to drive successful strategy implementation in their organizations and the ways in which Diversity affects these components.

To create this center of Diversity excellence, diversity-mature individuals must be able to let go of hindering concepts, such as only people with good interpersonal skills can be successful in managing diversity. Good interpersonal skills help, but they are not the sole arbiters of success. Diversity-mature individuals are highly capable of unlearning when needed. Diversity effectiveness requires a willingness and ability to monitor both yourself and the environment, to challenge yourself regularly, and to devise specific ways to work with new concepts so that they eventually become second nature (Thomas, 1999).

D-BAM: Diversity Business Alignment Maps

To create excellence in performance (utilizing diversity), diversity professionals must possess core Diversity skills, which are implemented from a strategic framework. These skills, among others, include the following:

- *Ability to identify diversity mixtures and their related tensions.* Because unidentified mixtures cannot be addressed, this is a critical skill. On the surface this skill seems simple and straightforward, yet according to Thomas (1999), many people fail to master it. There is a natural tendency to focus on the diversity mixture that is of most interest to them and to ignore the others. People often overemphasize one Diversity dimension such as race or gender at the expense of identifying a critical mixture that may have the most impact on organizational performance.
- *Ability to analyze mixtures and related tensions.* Not all mixtures need to be addressed, only those that interfere with achieving the goal. How key is the mixture? How disruptive are the tensions? Is any action needed? If action is taken, will it significantly enhance meeting the organizational objectives?
- *Ability to select an appropriate response.* If action is needed, what should the action be? In *Redefining Diversity* (1996), Thomas suggests responses from a

D-BAM: Diversity Business Alignment Maps

framework that identifies at least eight choices, including increase/decrease, deny, assimilate, suppress, isolate, tolerate, build future relationships or foster mutual adaptation. Diversity professionals who are skilled in using these responses can quickly sort through the possible options and select the most effective one.

To be effective, Diversity professionals must demonstrate a kind of diversity maturity that allows them to internalize key Diversity concepts and use them to guide their actions along with integrating the core skills.

Similarly, to be effective at Diversity measurement, individuals aiming for greater Diversity measurement effectiveness would do well to ask themselves some critical personal questions:

- Am I comfortable with working with metrics and evaluating data from all demographic groups?
- Are there concepts around measuring diversity, especially beyond race and gender, that I struggle to accept? If so, how have I attempted to overcome my biases?
- How will my comfort or lack of comfort with metrics affect my ability to utilize them within this workplace?
- Do I enjoy Diversity measurement? If so, what kind? If so, how much?

D-BAM: Diversity Business Alignment Maps

- Do I need to hire someone to conduct this portion of our strategic Diversity impact analysis or simply support our efforts as a reviewer?
- Do I really want to do the real work required to rigorously apply Diversity measures and following the Diversity return-on-investment (DROI®) process through to its conclusion?

Answers to these questions will help identify any baseline resistance to the Diversity measurement process. Sometimes biases toward diversity measurement can come from within our profession and impede setting standards of excellence.

To sustain Diversity professionals' momentum for excellence and measurement, communities of practice are required. What is a Diversity measurement community of practice? It is a group of people who share a concern, set of problems, or a passion for identifying the impact of diversity using measurement processes and who deepen their knowledge and expertise in this area by learning about Diversity measurement and interacting on an ongoing basis. They find it useful to compare designs regularly and to discuss the intricacies of their area of interest in Diversity measurement. Currently, the Hubbard Diversity Measurement and Productivity Institute (HDM&P) and the Hubbard Diversity Return on Investment Institutes operate communities of practice focused

D-BAM: Diversity Business Alignment Maps

on Diversity analytics and ROI measurement called the Diversity Return on Investment (DROI) Forum.

As communities of practice, these people do not necessarily work together every day, but they meet as strategic business partners because they find value in their interactions. As they spend time together, they typically share information, insight, and advice. They help each other solve problems. They discuss their diversity measurement situations, their aspirations, and their needs. They ponder issues, explore ideas, and act as sounding boards. They may create tools, standards, generic designs, manuals, and other documents. However they accumulate knowledge, they become informally bound by the value they find in learning about diversity measurement together. This value is not merely instrumental for their work. It also accrues in personal satisfaction of knowing colleagues who understand each other's perspectives and of belonging to a group of people who enjoy the diversity measurement work. Over time, they develop a unique perspective on the topic as well as a body of common knowledge, practices, and approaches. They may even develop a common sense of identity (Wenger, McDermott, Snyder, 2002). They become a diversity measurement community of practice.

D-BAM: Diversity Business Alignment Maps

Final Thoughts

An effective, measurable business case for Diversity must be built on a solid framework of both concept and science through the work of competent, credible Diversity professionals using clear standards of excellence linked to business performance. They must view Diversity as an integral part of the organizational system. By integrating the ideas underlying Diversity with specific measurement strategies and organizational systems theory, Diversity professionals can help the organization examine and utilize its diverse resources more dynamically. It is, of course, impossible to predict future events and results; however, we can make better decisions for the future by using tools such as the Diversity Scorecard to guide us and to test alternatives as a basis for discussing how the future might look.

References

Addison Reid, Barbara. "Mentorships Ensure Equal Opportunity." *Personnel Journal*, November 1994, 122–123.

Baytos, Lawrence M. *Designing & Implementing Successful Diversity Programs*. Englewood Cliffs, NJ: Prentice Hall, 1995.

Becker, Brian E., Mark A. Huselid, and Dave Ulrich. *The HR Scorecard: Linking People, Strategy, and Performance*. Boston: Harvard Business School Press, 2001.

D-BAM: Diversity Business Alignment Maps

Capowski, Genevieve. "Managing Diversity." *Management Review*, 85: 13–19.

Cox, Taylor Jr. *Cultural Diversity in Organizations*. San Francisco: Berrett-Koehler, 1993.

Cox, Taylor, Jr., and Ruby L Beale. *Developing Competency to Manage Diversity*. San Francisco: Berrett-Koehler, 1997.

Davis, Drew. "Beyond Casual Fridays: Are Managers Tuned in to Workplace Culture?" *Canadian HR Reporter*, May 6, 1996, 17.

Haskett, James L., Thomas O. Jones, Gary W. Loveman, Earl W. Sasser, Jr., and Leonard A Schlesinger. "Putting the Service-Profit Chain to Work." *Harvard Business Review*, March/April 1994, 164–174.

Haskett, James L., Earl W. Sasser, Jr., and Leonard A. Schlesinger. *The Service Profit Chain*. New York: The Free Press, 1997.

Hubbard, Edward E. *How to Calculate Diversity Return on Investment*. Petaluma, CA: Global Insights, 1999.

Hubbard, Edward E. *Measuring Diversity Results*. Petaluma, CA: Global Insights, 1997.

IBM and Towers Perrin. *Priorities for Competitive Advantage*. New York: IBM and Towers Perrin, 1991.

Kaplan, Robert S., and David P. Norton. *The Balanced Scorecard*. Boston: Harvard Business School Press, 1996.

Lapp, Janet. *Plant Your Feet Firmly in Mid-Air*. Albany, NY: Delmar, 1996.

Loden, Marilyn. *Implementing Diversity*. Chicago: Irwin, 1996.

D-BAM: Diversity Business Alignment Maps

Loden, Marilyn, and Judith Rosener. *Workforce America.* Homewood, IL: Business One Irwin, 1991.

Martinez, Michelle Neely. "Equality Effort: Sharpens Bank's Edge." *HR Magazine*, January 1995, 38–43.

Poole, Phebe-Jane. *Diversity: A Business Advantage.* Ajax, Ontario: Poole Publishing, 1997.

Reichheld, Frederick F., and Earl W. Sasser, Jr. "Zero Defections: Quality Comes to Services." *Harvard Business Review*, October 1990.

Rucci, Anthony J., Steven P. Kirn, and Richard T. Quinn. "The Employee-Customer-Profit Chain at Sears." *Harvard Business Review*, 76(1):1998, 90.

Thomas, R. Roosevelt, Jr. *Beyond Race and Gender.* New York: AMACOM, 1991.

Thomas, R. Roosevelt, Jr. *Building a House for Diversity.* New York: AMACOM, 1999.

Thomas, R. Roosevelt, Jr. *Redefining Diversity.* New York: AMACOM, 1996.

See "No More Business as Usual," *Working Woman*, Special Advertising Section: Strength Through Diversity for Bottom-line Success: A Call to Manage Diversity. MacDonald Communications Corporation, March 1999.

Von Eron, Ann M. "Ways to Assess Diversity Success." *HR Magazine*, August 1995, 51–60.

Wenger, Etienne, Richard McDermott, and William M. Snyder. *Cultivating Communities of Practice.* Boston: Harvard Business School Press, 2002.

Chapter Three: Building a Diversity D-BAM to Tell Your Impact Story

The Power of Diversity ROI (DROI®) Measurement Alignment

Misaligned metrics, like cars out of alignment, can develop serious problems if they are not corrected quickly. Like the cars, they are hard to steer and don't respond well to changes in direction. Alignment is a response to the new business reality where organizational business requirements are in flux and competitive forces are turbulent, and the bonds of employee loyalty and engagement can be challenging. Old "representation-focused" approaches to Diversity metrics are not strategic or performance-driven.

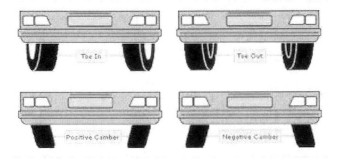

D-BAM: Diversity Business Alignment Maps

A familiar criticism of Diversity and Inclusion metrics is that they are often put together in a piecemeal fashion without a clear framework of how they are relevant to the current and future business needs of the organization. Many Diversity and Inclusion interventions have the best intentions, but they sometimes lack this **"alignment or linkage"** to the firm's overall strategic direction. A great majority of the measurement approaches tend to focus primarily on "activities" rather than "evidence-based outcomes and targeted results." They are usually not built on comprehensive business needs assessments that are targeted to solve real business challenges.

I am fond of saying that **"focusing on tactics without a strategic framework is like learning to run faster in the wrong direction."** You cannot make a strategic contribution without a tight alignment and linkage to the business objectives and success metrics of the organization. Crafting a well-thought out Diversity Business Alignment Map (D-BAM) ensures your Diversity and Inclusion strategies are tight and on target. It helps you clearly "tell your Diversity and Inclusion impact story" in a "one-page" graphic illustration demonstrating how your Diversity and Inclusion initiatives drive bottom-line business outcomes linked to the Mission and Vision of the organization.

If you want to have your interventions resonate with the C-suite and line managers, they must be based in the real bottom-line

D-BAM: Diversity Business Alignment Maps

needs that drive organizational performance. Whether it is Diversity training to teach cultural competency skills, selling products to emerging market clientele, innovating new products and services for a global market, delivering health care services, serving governmental constituents, meeting a wide range of student needs, etc., strategically aligned diversity measurement strategies have the best chance at success and sustainability.

Let's look at an example that helps to clarify this relationship.

First, among the organization's strategic objectives, you find a series of crucial performance areas. One of these focuses on an objective of improved customer service. Based upon the importance of this area to the business, the Diversity organization has created a corresponding strategic objective in the D-BAM to analyze and improve service across all demographic market segments.

In the second step, you determine that for service to be improved in these targeted markets, the critical success factor areas must include "improved communication," "culturally appropriate interactions," quick access, increased satisfaction and accurate information.

Finally, these critical success factor areas lead you to select Diversity performance measures and indicators that support each critical success factor area such as the "percentage of multilingual

D-BAM: Diversity Business Alignment Maps

service transactions delivered," "number of rings to answer," "percentage of favorable response on the diverse customer satisfaction survey, $ revenue increase due to diverse customer referrals" etc. This type of alignment drives improved performance and gains top management support.

What Is Top Management Support?

Top management support is not a speech or a memo; it is real actions taken by the leadership function in an organization that undergirds building a successful diverse and inclusive work environment. It is not something nice that the president or CEO of the organization mentions in a speech. It is a continuing commitment backed up by words and deeds over a sustained period of time. It means a strong personal involvement on the part of management in shaping the Diversity vision and accountability of leaders, employees and others. In a word, it requires commitment.

"**Diversity Leadership Commitment**" can be defined as demonstrated evidence and actions taken by leaders to support, challenge and champion the Diversity process within their organization. It reflects the degree to which the organization's leaders utilize behaviors that set the Diversity vision, direction and policy into actual practice. It also reflects the individual level and degrees of accountability leaders have in forging an

D-BAM: Diversity Business Alignment Maps

implementation strategy, and it analyzes the level of specific behavior they exhibit as a model Diversity champion.

From an organizational change point of view, Diversity Leadership Commitment is the behavior that helps establish a direction or goal for change (a vision), provides a sense of urgency and importance for the vision, facilitates the motivation of others, and cultivates necessary conditions for achieving the vision. This spirit and essence must be reflected in the Diversity and Inclusion initiatives you develop in the D-BAM. Diversity Leadership Commitment is critical to the Diversity change process. It cannot be delegated or given just tacit consideration. It is clear that the CEO of the organization and heads of the main operating units have primary responsibility for breakthrough progress on Diversity. If they do not hold themselves accountable for the leadership requirements to execute Diversity initiatives, the change effort is doomed to failure.

Diversity officers and their staffs have a crucial role to play as facilitators of the Diversity change process. Leaders alone cannot be held responsible for making it happen. As a unifying force, Diversity Leadership Commitment throughout the organization serves as a key lynchpin for success that is combined with the efforts of others to sustain forward progress.

D-BAM: Diversity Business Alignment Maps

Defining diversity performance measures that help sustain alignment can be broken down into three steps: first, identifying specific Diversity objectives; second, determining where and how the organization must succeed to accomplish each Diversity performance objective, spelling out the "wheres" and "hows" as a set of critical success factor areas; and finally, selecting Diversity performance measures for each critical success factor area. These measures help determine if the organization is in fact performing well on its objectives. Diversity performance measures are the tools we use to determine whether we are meeting our objectives and moving toward the successful implementation of our strategy.

How Do You Begin the Alignment Process?

If you want to successfully align your Diversity measurement process with the business strategy of the organization, you can utilize a nine-step method to improve and effectively calibrate your work.

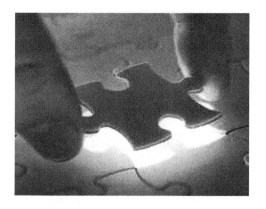

D-BAM: Diversity Business Alignment Maps

Step 1: Start Thinking of Diversity and Inclusion Metrics as a Critical Part of the Business.

It is important to discard the idea that Diversity and Inclusion is separate from the rest of the organization or can be addressed by simply implementing a series of well-intentioned activities. All Diversity interventions must be measured and integrated with the ongoing operational activities of the organization. It requires conducting an analysis to set as top priority those metrics that help the organization meet its strategic objectives.

It is also important to get copies of the organization's strategic business plans and mine them for ideas, impacts and consequences. Meet with key managers to talk about their plans. Determine where they will need Diversity and Inclusion support and ROI-based metrics to measure their success. You should also look for new technologies, organization changes, new product lines and new company directions.

Step 2: Learn the Business!

Knowing the business is critical to the alignment process. If you want to talk with managers coherently about their challenges, you must know the business and how it affects their business, especially the financial end. It is crucial to know things such as company earnings per share, net profit as a percent of sales, gross profit margin, net income, etc. It is important to talk with

D-BAM: Diversity Business Alignment Maps

colleagues in the accounting and strategic planning departments about the state of the business. Study the annual reports and anything else you can get your hands on until you are comfortable with the company's financial objectives and competitive position. Know the company's ROI numbers, sales figures, operating profit, debt-to-equity ratios and cash flows.

You should be conversant about new business ventures and the company's direction. Know your company's products and services. Learn what's selling, what's not and why. Alignment requires that you are able to identify with line management priorities to build understanding and credibility.

Step 3: Develop Measurement Strategies and Activities That Line Managers Want.

Start identifying business and line department priorities first, and then focus on Diversity and Inclusion priorities. This is called being other-centered. It improves the Diversity metrics alignment by creating a business context for developing analytics solutions. Use your study of strategic plans, operating reports and talks with line managers to locate an appropriate set of metrics to evaluate your diversity interventions. It is critical to get customer input and feedback on proposed initiatives.

D-BAM: Diversity Business Alignment Maps

Step 4: Involve Top Management.

Top management's involvement is critical to the alignment process. Therefore, it is important to interview them and ask what organizational needs they consider important. You must complete research at all levels of the organization to create a comprehensive measurement strategy.

Develop a master plan by department, level or position to focus your Diversity metrics strategy. This means conducting a utility analysis to determine which metrics are critical, important or nice to include to effectively assess the success of the Diversity or Inclusion intervention. Use leaders and managers as much as possible as subject matter experts versus your own process knowledge to gauge the performance gap that exists. Once the specific gap is known, an appropriate Diversity and/or Inclusion intervention can be designed.

Step 5: Develop Interventions that are Practical, How-To Approaches

A lot of organizations will say they have Diversity and Inclusion measures in place. However, when you actually check them, you see that they are activity counts. They'll look around and say they've established a council or have had a particular celebration on a particular day. And while those are important, senior leaders don't always see these things as bottom-line outcomes. They're not

D-BAM: Diversity Business Alignment Maps

looking at how the Diversity process increased market penetrations in key ethnic markets or how the Diversity process has added 'X' number of customers. Progressive companies show how they have utilized diversity and inclusion technologies to integrate Diversity process into productivity improvement issues, product quality issues and innovation challenges.

To have credibility, Diversity interventions reflected in the D-BAM must be developed in a way that seamlessly integrate with key organizational priorities at critical levels and are designed in a way that employees can use them right away to improve the organization's functioning. To accomplish this, it may require having the flexibility to move away from pure "academic images" of Diversity and Inclusion theory and venture into the realm of the "live-lab" of real organizational problems and challenges. It means working "hand-in-hand" with line managers as strategic business partners to solve some of the messy problems of performance improvement and change. As Diversity and Inclusion professionals, we must ask ourselves…who am I developing this intervention for…to go along with the latest fad that other organizations are using or for my internal (or external) clients to help solve their real business challenges? These challenges must be verified with an effective Business Needs Analysis in order to show the benefits and ROI impact.

D-BAM: Diversity Business Alignment Maps

It is important to stay clear of theories and fads that are not strategically tied to producing organization-enhancing results. Sure, some of them can help create "out-of-the-box" thinking that may help produce new, practical approaches that could generate value. However, these ideas need to be well researched and tested for their practical strategic value and potential impact.

It is also critical to limit "Diversity and Inclusion speak" when working with internal clients and sponsors. As Diversity and Inclusion professionals, we should know the nuances of Diversity and Inclusion processes; however your audience does not have to be masters of it. It may take a while to gain credibility from their vantage point. This credibility will come faster when you are able to demonstrate specific, measurable results in quantitative and qualitative terms. The results and outcomes of the Diversity initiatives reflected in the D-BAM must show how the results are tied to the organization's bottom-line impact. The results you obtain will improve your level of credibility, commitment and involvement, not the merits of theories and fads alone.

Step 6: Get a Handle on Diversity R.O.I. (DROI®)

DROI® is a registered trademark of Hubbard & Hubbard, Inc. All rights reserved.

It is absolutely essential to master the technologies of Diversity ROI (DROI®) analytics and measurement processes for all of the

D-BAM: Diversity Business Alignment Maps

interventions you provide. It is critical to identify interventions, programs, and activities that have a measurable impact on organizational performance.

I have always thought of Diversity and Inclusion as professional disciplines and fields of study. However, if it is to be taken seriously as a discipline and field of study, it must possess a structure, framework and critical components that are consistent with other serious disciplines.

For example, if we examine the disciplines of Marketing, Sales Operations, and the like, we would find they all have well-defined competencies, proven theories, and applied sciences that under gird their application. These theories and sciences provide a recognized structure, strategy and a set of measurable standards to guide those who work in the field.

If we examine the disciplines that include doctors, engineers, lawyers, and others, they must be certified to practice their craft. There are also certifications for human resource professionals such as the PHR and SPHR certifications offered by the Society for Human Resource Management (SHRM) for Human Resource Professionals, the HPI certification for Trainers by the American Society for Training and Development (ASTD), or the CPT certification for Organization Development professionals offered by the International Society for Performance Improvement (ISPI).

D-BAM: Diversity Business Alignment Maps

The Hubbard Diversity Return on Investment (DROI®) Institute offers seven Diversity and Inclusion certifications based in its Diversity ROI® and Diversity ROI Analytics® methodologies:

- Certified Diversity ROI Professional® (CDRIP)
- Certified Diversity Trainer® (CDT)
- Certified Diversity Advisor® (CDA)
- Certified Diversity Performance Consultant® (CDPC)
- Certified Diversity Business Partner® (CDBP)
- Certified Diversity Strategist® (CDS)
- Certified Diversity Intervention Specialist® (CDIS)

These fields of study contain specific, identifiable roles that are performed, areas of expertise that allow a practitioner to build specialized concentrations of skills and knowledge within the discipline, detailed outputs produced by these roles, as well as a model of measurable competencies that define specific behaviors that enable the work to be completed with a high degree of accuracy and effectiveness. These skills and competencies are foundational components to acquire and sustain the ability to build an effective D-BAM.

As a professional discipline, Diversity ROI (DROI®) practices must align with key objectives and outcomes to operate with similar standards built on a solid framework of both concept and science. These practices must be delivered through the work of

D-BAM: Diversity Business Alignment Maps

competent, credible Diversity and Inclusion professionals using clear standards of excellence linked to business performance. Using our talents and skills, based upon a competency-rich Diversity Discipline Framework™, Diversity professionals will be able to integrate the ideas underlying Diversity and Inclusion with specific measurement strategies and organizational systems theory to create a Diversity and Inclusion-enriched climate that utilizes diverse resources more effectively. Getting a handle on ROI means identifying units of measure for the interventions and activities that have a measurable impact on performance. We must consistently apply measurement sciences, track our interventions, and publish them as Diversity ROI (DROI®) studies such that they can be utilized as "best practices".

Sample measures which support a Diversity ROI (DROI®) measurement alignment strategy include covering key Diversity Scorecard perspectives such as:

Workforce Profile Perspective

- Diversity Hit Rate
- #/ % Minorities as Officials and Managers
- #/% Diversity Survival and Loss Rate
- #/% Turnover by Length of Service

D-BAM: Diversity Business Alignment Maps

Workplace Climate and Culture Profile Perspective

- % Favorable Ratings on Cultural Audit Demographic Group
- "Employer of Choice" Ratings versus Top 5- 10 Competitors
- Retention Rates of Critical Human Capital
- # and Type of Policies and Procedures Assessed for Diverse Workforce Impact

It is important to design evaluations and utilize metrics that are practical and reflect a systemic analysis. For example, use before and after measures which examine Diversity and Inclusion intervention results compared to key measures which are already established and utilized in the organization.

It is also imperative that you are cautious and careful with the procedure to demonstrate how you isolated the Diversity ROI value from all other possible interventions (that could have contributed to the organizational benefit). Be careful what you take credit for. In a Diversity ROI (DROI®) study, it is important that you only list those outcomes you can control which demonstrate a "chain-of-impact" to the outcome. Diversity and Inclusion intervention outputs are "inputs" that fuel contributions to line results. There are usually many intervening variable in the outcome production process. Isolation techniques must include

D-BAM: Diversity Business Alignment Maps

utilizing scientific processes such as control groups, time-series analysis, forecast estimates, etc., to attribute Diversity and Inclusion's contribution to specific business outcomes and benefits (separate and apart from other contributors).

Step 7: Make Some "Hard-Nose" Decisions About What is Needed

It is essential to conduct a comprehensive Business Assessment or "Needs Analysis" to determine what interventions are necessary to meet the intent of the aligned business objectives. For example, when evaluating an organizational challenge, a practitioner may be partial to a favorite Diversity or Inclusion intervention regardless of the problem or need. It is crucial that a scientific approach is taken where effective data collection helps determine the appropriate response, not what the practitioner favors. Performing a comprehensive Needs Analysis is the cornerstone of implementing a solid, credible performance improvement process. It helps practitioners make "hard-nosed" decisions and provides an appropriate justification for either developing or not developing a Diversity or Inclusion intervention. We *must* conduct a needs analysis, no matter how abbreviated, before any intervention development takes place.

If a Diversity Training intervention is required, for example, the objectives of the Needs Analysis are to:

D-BAM: Diversity Business Alignment Maps

- Describe the *exact nature* of a performance discrepancy
- Determine the *cause(s)* of the discrepancy
- Recommend the appropriate *solution(s)*
- Describe the *learner population*

In general, Needs Analysis consists of the following steps.

- **Step 1:** Identify and describe the business and performance discrepancies.
- **Step 2:** Determine the causes of the discrepancies.
- **Step 3:** Identify those performance discrepancies that are based on lack of skill or knowledge. Then identify the skills and knowledge needed that is related to diversity and diversity competence.
- **Step 4:** Determine whether diversity training or another intervention is a viable solution.
- **Step 5:** Recommend solutions.
- **Step 6:** Describe the performer's and organization's role in behaviorally specific terms that relate to diversity excellence and performance.

D-BAM: Diversity Business Alignment Maps

How Are Diversity Training Analysis and Evaluation Linked to Diversity Measurement Alignment?

A needs analysis establishes the criteria for measuring the success of training after its completion. A thorough needs analysis should answer the question:

"What good _will_ training do?"

A thorough Diversity ROI training evaluation will answer the question:

"What good _did_ training do and what was the Return on Investment (DROI)?"

An effective Diversity ROI training evaluation **cannot** be conducted unless a thorough needs analysis has been completed. We cannot determine what was accomplished by a Diversity training intervention or program unless we have first defined what the program was **intended** to accomplish. The Diversity training needs analysis provides baseline measures against which to judge our Diversity training efforts and will help us make the hard-nosed decisions about what is the best way to meet our internal/external client's need.

D-BAM: Diversity Business Alignment Maps

Step 8: Get Away From a Program Orientation

Diversity is not a program; it is a process of systemic organizational change. Programs have a beginning and an end. However, people will never be finished with their differences. Therefore Diversity interventions, shown in the D-BAM, and the metrics that support them must reflect a range that supports the systems and processes that drive real organizational performance. The context for Diversity performance is the organization's business and its objectives. To be relevant and aligned, it is critical to think in terms of the business, its goals, objectives and its performance needs. It requires Diversity and Inclusion practitioners connect to and work in concert with all levels of the organization.

It is reported that many top and senior executives truly support their Diversity organizations and process, but feel they should play a stronger strategic role in the growth and development of the organization. They expect Diversity and Inclusion practitioners to help increase productivity and provide solutions that generate a stronger competitive edge. In effect, both top and line managers are seeking Diversity professionals who can function as "strategic business partners" to solve real business problems which have a bottom-line impact on the organization's day-to-day and strategic priorities. To successfully align and link Diversity and Inclusion strategies with the organization's strategic business plan, you must

D-BAM: Diversity Business Alignment Maps

actively pursue top and line managers regarding their specific business problems and speak their language. For example, if we are working with the Finance department, we must be able to talk about their problems and potential solutions using Diversity and Inclusion in financial terms, impacts and consequences. If the problem is focused in the operations area, we must talk in operational terms, etc.

Step 9: Stick With It!

Developing a Diversity ROI (DROI®) measurement capability is a "skill". And like any skill we must learn what it is, understand its applications, use it, study the feedback from its use and refine the skill until we build a level of competency. This is an expectation for anyone that offers themselves up as an "expert" in a particular discipline or field of study. We expect doctors, engineers, social scientists, technicians, etc., to have mastered their craft in order to trust the solutions and alternatives they suggest. The same is true for Diversity professionals. We must hold ourselves to a high standard whether or not our C-Suite executives and others ask for it.

A critical element of meeting that standard is a strategic alignment with the strategy, structures and systems that drive the organization's performance. It is imperative to take advantage of learning and listening opportunities that broaden our

D-BAM: Diversity Business Alignment Maps

understanding, build Diversity ROI capability as well as business acumen.

It's not easy. It will take a lot of work and a heavy persistence for excellence at your craft. It requires that we possess an internal standard that says we do not accept being mediocre at our craft. Developing this expertise won't happen overnight or without setbacks and frustrations, but it can be done and is worth the struggle. This means that as Diversity and Inclusion professionals we must develop our D-BAMs with a "strategic alignment mindset" that places our Diversity ROI (DROI®) measurement efforts on par with any discipline that drives business results and success Without this tight alignment of strategy and process, our interventions and initiatives will not be seen as a credible and compelling way to get the organization's business done!

References

Hubbard, Edward E., Diversity Training ROI: How to Measure the Return on Investment of Diversity Training Initiatives, Global Insights Publishing, Petaluma, California, 2010

Chapter Four: The Value Creation Process

Creating Value Enterprise-wide

The Diversity Business Alignment Map drives the process for transforming diverse intangible asset capabilities into tangible customer and financial outcomes. It provides executives with a framework for describing, executing, and managing the Diversity and Inclusion strategy in a knowledge-based economy.

This diagram illustrates the sample architecture of a basic enterprise-wide strategy map. The cause-and-effect logic of this design constitutes the hypotheses of the strategy. The financial perspective contains two themes—growth and productivity—for improving shareholder value. The value proposition in the customer perspective clearly emphasizes the importance of delivering measurable value for the productivity and growth strategies shown in the Map. Four strategic themes in the internal perspective—Operations Excellence, Diverse Customer Management, Innovation and Workplace Excellence drive the means to have impact on the two primary themes. The Operations Excellence and Diverse Customer Management processes allow the Diversity organization to help drive the "Productivity" theme.

D-BAM: Diversity Business Alignment Maps

The Innovation and Workplace Excellence processes allow the diversity organization to help drive the "Growth" theme.

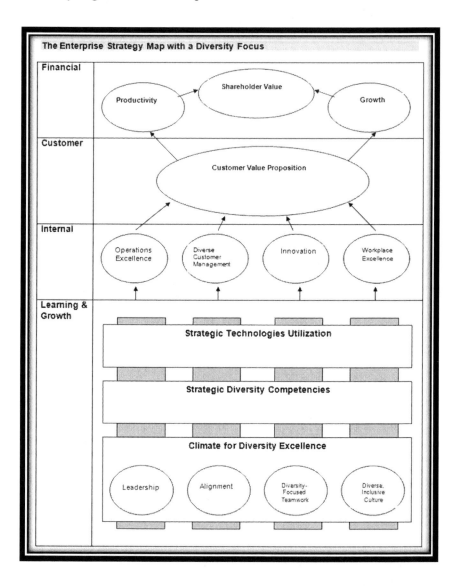

D-BAM: Diversity Business Alignment Maps

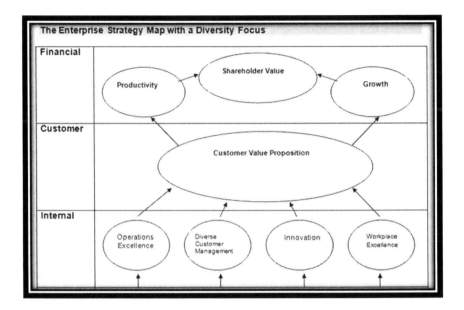

The learning and growth perspective identifies the intangible assets that are most important to the strategy. The objectives in this perspective identify key leadership roles to ensure effective management and leadership throughout the organization, strengthen strategic alignment, build a diverse talented team, and integrate critical processes and behaviors to generate a diverse and inclusive culture.

D-BAM: Diversity Business Alignment Maps

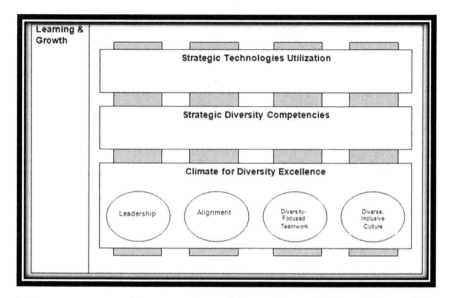

It lays out a core framework to fully utilize additional intangible resources such as Strategic Technologies, Strategic Diversity Competencies reflected in the diverse human capital experiences that provide invaluable information and resource inputs to problems and opportunities.

This basic enterprise D-BAM can serve as a helpful template to begin mapping out your strategic approach to demonstrate the *"unique and sustainable ways by which the Diversity and Inclusion organization will create value for the organization"*. Templates, strategic themes, and intangible assets are the building blocks for understanding and executing strategy. They provide increased granularity for executives to describe and manage strategy at an operational level of detail.

D-BAM: Diversity Business Alignment Maps

Integrating "Value Creation" in a D-BAM by applying effective Diversity and Inclusion initiatives and metrics is a framework for success that empowers organization executives and leaders to better understand and manage their firm's most valuable asset – their people. When an organization's corporate and Diversity and Inclusion values are in alignment with their "People Brand Promise" value is created in the form of brand equity and that brand equity can be leveraged to drive sustainable competitive advantage and superior financial performance.

Inclusion, for example, is the invisible thread that ties the elements of an organization's culture together. It helps to promote open communication, knowledge sharing and innovation by creating a collegial, mutually respectful environment. It allows workers to bring their full capabilities to bear in the workplace by fostering a unified culture of acceptance and idea utilization.

I define inclusiveness as *"the act or process of using the information, tools, skills, insights, and other talents that each individual has to offer that results in the measurable, mutual benefit and gain of everyone."* It also includes providing everyone with opportunities to contribute their thoughts, ideas, and concerns. If present, inclusiveness results in people feeling valued and respected. When applied effectively, "Inclusiveness" results in increased engagement, improved product, service delivery, and enhanced financial performance.

D-BAM: Diversity Business Alignment Maps

Therefore, it makes sense that programs promoting inclusion have a measurable impact on an organization's bottom line and on workforce productivity. Not long ago, the Institute for Corporate Productivity's (i4cp) released an Inclusion Measurement study that addressed some of the measurement issues relating to Inclusion and the bottom-line. This study was released as part of its "Inclusion Measurement: Policies and Practices of High-Performance Organizations" report, which found a 14 percent gap between high- and low-performing organizations — 22 percent compared to 8 percent — when it comes to the use of productivity data in determining inclusion success.

The goal of the study was to determine how high-performance organizations are approaching the Inclusion challenge and how they are measuring success. A high-performance designation was based on i4cp's Market Performance Index (MPI), which is identified through a series of questions that determine a company's current performance in revenue growth, market share, profitability and customer satisfaction versus those same items five years ago.

Make Measurement Follow Initiatives

The aforementioned finding on productivity as a metric for Inclusion success demonstrates increased interest among higher-performing organizations in evidence-based human resources

D-BAM: Diversity Business Alignment Maps

(EBHR). EBHR is driven by the need for more stringent HR metrics that are relevant to business goals and the bottom line.

The study showed that, though 62 percent of organizations overall reported that one driver of Inclusion initiatives is to increase productivity and engagement, only 15 percent of respondents reported using productivity data to assess the success of those efforts. This begs the question: How are the other organizations going to know if they have addressed the driving forces behind their Inclusion program's goals and objectives? Based on supplemental interviews and focus groups conducted by i4cp, the answer is either the business case for Inclusion has yet to be made in those organizations or the case was made based on inspirational ('faith-based") definitions and drivers for the Inclusion initiative that don't lend themselves to measurement.

Experience of Inclusion

One of the keys to measuring this process is the experience of Inclusion. The *experience of Inclusion* is "individuals' perception of the extent to which they feel safe, trusted, accepted, respected, supported, valued, fulfilled, engaged, and authentic in their working environment, both as individuals and as members of particular identity groups" (Ferdman, Barrera, Allen, & Vuong, 2009) —in short, the psychological sense on the part of individuals that indeed they are being included. When an individual

D-BAM: Diversity Business Alignment Maps

experiences Inclusion, she or he feels fully present and involved, believes that others recognize and appreciate his or her contributions, and feels both safe and open about his or her social identities. In this conceptualization, components of the experience of Inclusion in work groups include involvement and engagement in the workgroup, the ability to be heard and to influence decision making, the feeling of being valued, a sense of authenticity or being able to bring one's whole self to work, and the sense that diversity is recognized, attended to, and honored (Ferdman, Barrera, et al., 2009).

Hubbard Inclusion ROI Metrics

How can a diversity executive report to the CEO or board of directors that the organization is now 5 percent more inclusive than the year before and quantify what effect that statement has on the bottom line? In the absence of direct measures, it's often necessary to rely on indirect observations to determine if goals are being achieved. Metrics such as engagement scores, retention rates, productivity measures and diversity representation at various tiers often must be combined to create a broader picture of an inclusion strategy's impact on the overall organizational culture.

In order to effectively create an "_evidence-based_" measure of "Inclusion", a multi-faceted approach must be used. There are several prerequisite to craft the process:

D-BAM: Diversity Business Alignment Maps

To measure Inclusion, diversity executives should:

1) **Review the current definition and drivers behind the organization's Inclusion initiative and make sure they describe the desired cultural effect as well as the employee behaviors expected to achieve the desired results.** Establishing a definition for inclusion that spells out some measurable elements and is understood across the entire organization can maintain focus and help develop metrics.

2) **Align the organization's Inclusion definition and drivers with strategic organizational goals.** If the organization needs to improve its talent pipeline, weave Inclusion initiatives into existing talent management functions. If increasing innovation is critical, promote inclusion programs that will facilitate knowledge sharing. Both of these goals may require raising awareness of the employment brand by competing to become an employer of choice.

3) **As organizational goals help to develop drivers, and drivers help to develop programs to support those goals, make sure you formally measure the initiative's impact to ensure your programs are having an effect. Select or develop metrics that circle back to align with the original drivers.** By carefully articulating outcomes, organizations can define measures that assess the impact of their Inclusion strategy. For a concept as

D-BAM: Diversity Business Alignment Maps

ephemeral as inclusion, multiple qualitative, quantitative, effectiveness and efficiency metrics may be required to imply success or indicate the need for a course change.

What we know is effective organizational management processes are based on a foundation of effective measurement practices and almost everything else is based upon that. Organizations can be viewed as a conglomeration of many systems combined together to achieve a strategic value-related purpose. Measurement is actually the most fundamental system of all. The measurement system, for better or worse, triggers virtually everything that happens in an organization. This includes both its strategic and tactical actions.

This is due to the fact that all of the other organizational systems are ultimately based on what the measurement system is telling the other systems to do. No organization can be any better than its measurement system. If the measurement system works well, management practices will tend to drive the right things and the desired result will be achieved. Similarly, if the measurement system is designed or works poorly, management practices will tend to encourage dysfunctional behavior and drive failed execution.

D-BAM: Diversity Business Alignment Maps

Importance of Strategic Diversity ROI Measurement and Value Creation

The ultimate success of an organizational change management strategy greatly depends on how the change is introduced and implemented, rather than on the merit of the strategy itself. Successful development and utilization of key Diversity Return on Investment (ROI) measures is determined often by how well selected measures support the following:

1. Partnerships with all demographic groups such as staff, unions, key suppliers, customers, etc.

2. Transfer of power to front line employees who drive critical organizational processes

3. Integration of measurement, reporting and improvement of performance that results in "evidence-based" outcomes and action.

4. Linkage of performance measures to the organization's strategy and objectives.

Well-crafted strategic Diversity ROI measurements can help accomplish the following:

- Cut through the insignificant minutia and get right to the point. People can (and often do) advance their points of view about Diversity and other things with incredible

D-BAM: Diversity Business Alignment Maps

vagueness until they are challenged "to measure it". If the challenge is accepted, suddenly the focus shifts to generating clarity of purpose that has a basis in evidence and fact.

- It makes performance visible. Even if you can't see performance directly, you can see it indirectly using Diversity ROI-based measurement practices. This involves the concept of building "operational definitions". They are a critical part of any effective measurement process and will help provide a conceptual framework for understanding contributions such as "intangible diversity outcomes" that cannot be quantified into a financial or numeric equivalent.
- It tells you what you need to manage in the D-BAM's Strategic Diversity initiatives in order to get the results you want. Using "Diversity ROI measurement linkage maps" you will be able to identify, understand, and discuss the high leverage relationships that drive results, and apply them towards your organization's benefit.
- Diversity ROI Measurement makes accountability possible. It is difficult to hold yourself or anyone else, for that matter; accountable for something that is not being measured because there is no way to determine that whatever it is you were supposed to do has actually been accomplished. The D-BAM and your measurement

D-BAM: Diversity Business Alignment Maps

strategy tells you whether you (your employees or the organization) are doing the right things at the right times which is the essence of accountability.

- The D-BAM and Diversity ROI measurement analytics lets people know whether they are off track so that they can do something to correct their performance. Without your D-BAM and measurement strategy, feedback is often too vague and too late – and feedback that is too vague and too late is useless.

- The D-BAM and your Diversity ROI measurement strategy tells employees in the organization what is important. If you don't measure it, people won't pay attention to it. A person I met while working with a Navy client stated it this way: "people tend to do what you 'inspect' not always what you 'expect'. The D-BAM and your Diversity ROI measurement strategy set the foundation for what's important. This also highlights a critical reason why Diversity metrics and analytics must go well beyond 'representation-based' measurements. Diversity ROI measurements and analytics must focus on full business and operational processes such that the Diversity initiatives help drive your organization's mission.

- Using The D-BAM and your Diversity ROI metrics makes things happen; they are the antidote to inertia. I am

D-BAM: Diversity Business Alignment Maps

sure you have witnessed at some point in your career how milestones in a project plan get people on the project team energized towards a goal, while open-ended timeframes ultimately lead to complacency and low energy. If you give people an overarching roadmap (the D-BAM) and measurable Diversity ROI goals, you will help them track and monitor their efforts to make substantial progress.

- Diversity ROI measurement results in consequences (rewards and punishment) that further reinforce the inherent power of measurement. Any effective system of rewards and recognition, and any system of performance management must be based upon a solid foundation of measurement and strategy (the D-BAM).

- In general, executing Diversity and Inclusion with the D-BAM and your Diversity ROI measurement in mind helps you understand what is happening in the organization regarding the execution and impact of your organization's strategic direction which allows you to create added value. Utilizing a D-BAM and strategic Diversity ROI measurement enables you to make comparisons, study trends, and identify important correlations and causal relationships that will help establish a roadmap for success.

D-BAM: Diversity Business Alignment Maps

Current observations of those using a D-BAM and strategic Diversity ROI measurements reflect good news and bad news. The good news is that some organizations are finally discovering the importance of having a well-crafted D-BAM strategy and Diversity ROI metrics. The bad news is that most organizations are still using them very poorly or not at all beyond mere representation-based initiatives and analytics. In some cases, I have witnessed organizations investing millions of dollars in Diversity and Inclusion programs with "No" "Needs Analysis", or concrete ROI-based tracking and evaluation process or measurement strategy to gauge its effectiveness and impact. When this happens, Diversity organizations have little to offer to demonstrate their value and often suffer devastating consequences to their departments and their credibility in the organization.

Creating the Proper Measurement Environment for Success

Unfortunately, when used poorly, not only does Diversity performance measurement not live up to its promise, it can be an extremely negative force in the organization. Almost everyone has, at one time or another, experienced "negative measurement" used to expose negative things – errors, defects, accidents, cost overruns, exceptions of all kinds to trigger negative emotions like fear, threat, fault-finding, blame, and punishment. They also know how dangerous measurement can be in the hands of those who

D-BAM: Diversity Business Alignment Maps

don't use it well or benevolently. Although negative measurement can get results, it is mostly short-term compliance, and leaves a bad taste in people's mouths. For many employees, measurement is viewed, at best, as a 'necessary evil'. When this happens, the D-BAM strategic intent is lost and people often go into a "duck and cover mode".

Even worst, it is seen as a menacing force that is greeted with about the same enthusiasm as a "root canal"! When people think of strategy and performance measurement in this way, they think of being watched, being timed, being treated unfairly.

The environment of executing strategy and Diversity and Inclusion measurement has a major influence on how Diversity and Inclusion is perceived by employees and, therefore, how they respond emotionally to it. Since measurement, in general, is such an emotionally-laden topic, preparing the environment in which the D-BAM strategy and ROI measurement is conducted is an important requirement. Even if people aren't directly involved in the measurement, almost everyone feels strongly about it and its implication on them in the future.

Strategy and the measurements to support them are powerful. One of its primary purposes is to act as an effective communications tool. When implemented and managed properly, the D-BAM and ROI measurement strategy can strategically drive results. Most

D-BAM: Diversity Business Alignment Maps

employees seem to intuitively understand that most effective decisions will be made on the basis of having good, clear data provided by a well-designed D-BAM and ROI measurement strategy system. Although seldom explicitly acknowledged as such, the D-BAM and the ROI measurement strategy are important to people because they know that their success, their rewards, their budgets, their punishments and a host of other things ultimately are, directly or indirectly based on how well they execute the D-BAM strategy and drive ROI metrics and analytics.

To create value and a transformative ROI measurement-based environment, it is critical to address the following four key elements during your implementation process:

- **Context** – The context is everything that surrounds the D-BAM and Diversity ROI metrics task, including the social and psychological climate needed to drive employee behavior to execute processes in alignment with the D-BAM strategy and use the Diversity ROI measurement system. The context of measurement tends to reflect how the D-BAM and Diversity measurement is perceived by employees and therefore how well they will be used.
- **Focus** – Focus is what gets measured in the organization, that is, the Diversity analytics and measures themselves. Selecting the right Diversity analytics and measures can

D-BAM: Diversity Business Alignment Maps

create leverage and focus the organization on what is most important.

- **Integration** – Integration is how the D-BAM and Diversity ROI measures are related to each other, the relationship among the measures and strategic initiatives. Measurement frameworks make sure that the D-BAM and Diversity ROI measures relate to each other and are not just isolated metrics and strategies.

- **Interactivity** – Interactivity is the social interaction and employee involvement process around the D-BAM strategy and Diversity ROI measurement data. Interactivity is the key to transforming the D-BAM strategy and the Diversity and Inclusion measurement data information into "**applied**" operational knowledge and wisdom.

It is essential that all four keys work in tandem with one another. For example, without the right focus, other keys will be meaningless -- because if you don't have a D-BAM-like strategy and measure the right things, you won't be able to manage the right things because you won't get the right results – no matter how well you measure them technically. On the other hand, even with the right focus, without a positive context, people won't be motivated to measure the right things, will tend to focus on what will bring them the largest personal rewards, and will tend to have

D-BAM: Diversity Business Alignment Maps

an adversarial position towards whatever it is that is measured. When measurement has the wrong focus and a negative climate and cultural context, a multitude of things can go wrong.

Without the right integration, the D-BAM and the Diversity ROI measures will stand alone, functional silos will be perpetuated, individuals and functions will not be properly aligned, and there will be a natural tendency to maximize individual measures, often at the expense of other parts of the organization or the organization as a whole. In more advanced cases, individual measures may actually work against each other, and even cancel each other out.

Without frequent interaction relative to strategy and measurement, none of the other keys can really work. Without frequent and effective interactivity, you will have a technical engine without a social engine. In addition, you might develop a Diversity Business Alignment Map (D-BAM) or a Diversity scorecard ROI measurement framework, but who is going to maintain it and keep it updated? Without adequate interactivity, it is impossible to sustain any gains from the other three keys. This immediately begins to dilute your Value Creation efforts and impact.

When all four keys are working together synergistically utilizing an organization's D-BAM and Diversity ROI measurement system, amazing things can happen. Together, the four keys to powerful performance measurement will work in collaboration with each

D-BAM: Diversity Business Alignment Maps

other to enable the power of a DBAM and the Diversity ROI measurement framework to make a real, transformational difference in the organization's success!

References

"Using the Power of Inclusion ROI Metrics to Drive Performance and Organizational Brand Equity", Hubbard, Edward E., Diversity Executive Magazine, May 5, 2013.

"Unleashing the Strategic Power of Diversity ROI Measurement", Hubbard, Edward E., Diversity Executive Magazine, November 17, 2013

"Inclusion Measurement - Tracking the Intangible", Davis, Eric, i4cp, July 14, 2010.

Deane, Barbara and Ferdman, Bernardo, "Diversity at Work: The Practice of Inclusion", Josey-Bass, San Francisco, 2014.

Chapter Five: Aligning Intangible Assets to Business Strategy

Alignment: Intangible Assets Must Be Aligned with Strategy in Order to Create Value.

Intangible assets take on value only in the context of strategy, what they are expected to help the organization accomplish. For example, assume an organization wants to invest in staff training. Assume further that it has two choices—a training program on Lean Six-Sigma or a program on customer relationship management (CRM). Which program has the greatest value? Clearly the answer to this question depends on the organization's strategy. A company following a low total cost strategy, such as Dell and McDonald's, that needs to continually improve its operating processes would get higher value from Lean Six-Sigma training. A company such as Goldman Sachs or IBM Consulting, however, that follows a total customer solution strategy, would benefit most from CRM training. The same investment in training creates dramatically higher returns when it is aligned with the organization's strategy. Strategic alignment is the dominant principle in creating value from intangible assets.

D-BAM: Diversity Business Alignment Maps

Integration

The strategic role of intangible assets cannot be addressed on a stand-alone basis. An integrated program is required to support the enhancement of all the organization's intangible assets. When an organization groups its activities around functions, such as HR and IT, it often creates silos of specialization. People in separate functional departments often look to professional models within their disciplines as points of reference or benchmarks. Such specialization is obviously beneficial for creating deep functional excellence in each department. But, in practice, the different functional units strive for excellence in isolation from each other.

Each department competes for the organization's scarce resources; one argues to increase employee training while the other urges an expansion of technology capabilities. Solutions are sought in isolation and the results are usually disappointing. Investments in IT have no value unless complemented with HR and Diversity and Inclusion training as well as incentive programs. HR and Diversity and Inclusion training initiatives have little value unless complemented with modern technology tools. HR, Diversity and Inclusion, and IT investments must be integrated if the organization is to realize the full potential benefits. Alignment and integration provide the conceptual building blocks for developing objectives for diverse human capital, information capital, and organization capital in the learning and growth perspective.

D-BAM: Diversity Business Alignment Maps

Few organizations, however, exploit the potential competitive advantages from aligning and integrating their intangible assets. Kaplan and Norton conducted two surveys of HR and IT executives, to better understand their approaches to strategic alignment. Only one-third of the organizations reported strong alignment of HR and IT priorities with enterprise strategy.

Why the misalignment? Fundamental management processes designed to create alignment were not being used as intended. Few HR, Diversity and Inclusion, and IT organizations integrated planning with strategy, assigned relationship managers, or linked budgets to strategy. Executives do not dispute the need to align and integrate their intangible assets. Until now, however, they lacked a method for alignment and integration. In this chapter, we build upon internal process objectives we developed to describe how the D-BAM, Diversity ROI metrics, and critical analytics enable organizations to accomplish the following:

- Describe intangible assets
- Align and integrate intangible assets to the strategy
- Measure intangible assets and their alignment

Intangible assets have been described as "knowledge that exists in an organization to create a differential advantage" or "the capabilities of the company's diverse employees to satisfy diverse customer needs." Intangible assets encompass items such as

D-BAM: Diversity Business Alignment Maps

patents, copyrights, diverse workforce knowledge, leadership, information systems, and work processes. Kaplan and Norton, for example, examined the learning and growth perspective of several hundred strategy maps and Balanced Scorecards. Six objectives consistently appeared:

Human Capital

1. **Strategic competencies:** The availability of skills, talent, and know-how to perform activities required by the strategy. Kaplan and Norton found that about 80 percent of the scorecards included such an objective.

Information Capital

2. **Strategic information:** The availability of information systems and knowledge applications and infrastructure required to support the strategy. Kaplan and Norton found that about 80 percent of the scorecards included such an objective.

Organization Capital

3. **Culture:** Awareness and internalization of the shared mission, vision, and values needed to execute the strategy. Kaplan and Norton found that about 90 percent of the scorecards included such an objective.

D-BAM: Diversity Business Alignment Maps

4. **Leadership:** The availability of diverse, qualified leaders at all levels to mobilize the organizations toward their strategies. Kaplan and Norton found that about 90 percent of the scorecards included such an objective.

5. **Alignment:** Alignment of goals and incentives with the strategy at all organization levels. Kaplan and Norton found that about 70 percent of the scorecards included such an objective.

6. **Teamwork:** The sharing of knowledge and staff assets with strategic potential. Kaplan and Norton determined this objective was included in 60 percent of scorecards.

These objectives describe important intangible assets and provide a powerful framework for aligning and integrating them to the organization's strategy.

What does this all mean? Well, by using "Enterprise-wide D-BAM strategy maps", we can expect that organizations that manage its most important intangible assets can expect to become more tightly aligned to the overall organization's strategy. The D-BAM provides a clear framework for aligning human, information, and organization capital to the strategy, with sufficient specific detail to be meaningful, measurable, and actionable.

This step positions Diversity and Inclusion for success by aligning its intended outcome with the needs of the business. This

D-BAM: Diversity Business Alignment Maps

alignment is essential if the investment in a Diversity and Inclusion initiative is to reap a return. The term business is used to reflect important outcome measures (e.g., output, quality, cost, time) that exist in any setting, including governments, nonprofits, and nongovernmental organizations (NGOs).

The Importance of Business Alignment

Let's face it— not all programs are connected to the business. As mentioned earlier, the Diversity and Inclusion (D&I) function has a serious problem showing the value of D&I initiatives and programs, especially from a C-Suite point of view. New initiatives and programs are implemented based on the assumption that they are needed and will probably drive value.

This is essentially faith-based programming ("we have faith that this will work"). Unfortunately, many programs do not drive value, particularly those soft programs that are often initiated for the wrong reasons. The number one cause of a Diversity and Inclusion initiative's failure is the lack of business alignment at the outset and/or poor (or NO) Needs Analysis connection that validates (with evidence) the business need to undertake the initiative. New D&I initiatives and/or programs must begin with a clear focus on the desired outcomes. The end must be specified in terms of business measures so that the outcome— the actual improvement in the measures and the corresponding Diversity ROI are clear.

D-BAM: Diversity Business Alignment Maps

This establishes the expectations throughout the initiative analysis, design, development, delivery, and implementation stages. Beginning with the end in mind requires pinning down all the details to ensure that the program is properly planned and executed according to schedule. This up-front analysis is not always simple, as it requires a disciplined approach, one that adds credibility and allows for consistent application so that the analysis can be replicated.

A disciplined approach maintains process efficiency as various tools and templates are developed and used. This initial phase of analysis calls for focus and thoroughness, with little allowance for major shortcuts. Not every program should be subjected to the type of comprehensive analysis described in this chapter. Some needs are obvious and require little analysis other than that necessary to develop the initiative. For example, the need for a safety program usually translates into specific safety measures that need to improve. Additional analysis may be needed to confirm that the program addresses the perceived need and perhaps to fine-tune the program for future application.

The amount of analysis required often depends on the expected opportunity to be gained if the program is appropriate or the negative consequences anticipated if the program is inappropriate. When analysis is proposed, individuals may react with concern or resistance. Some Diversity practitioners are concerned about the

D-BAM: Diversity Business Alignment Maps

potential for "paralysis by analysis," where requests and directives lead only to additional analyses. These reactions can pose a problem for an organization, because analysis is necessary to ensure that a program is appropriate.

Unfortunately, analysis is often misunderstood— conjuring up images of complex problems, confusing models, and a deluge of data along with complicated statistical techniques to ensure that all bases are covered. In reality, analysis need not be so complicated. Simple techniques can uncover the cause of a problem or the need for a particular program and business as seen in the model below:

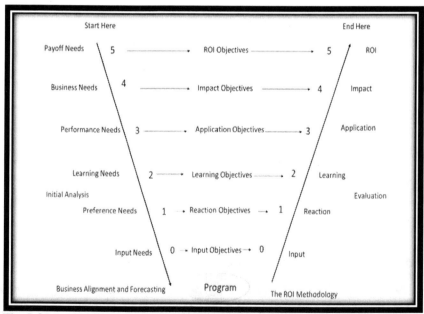

The ROI Institute Business Alignment "V" Model, Patricia P. Phillips, Jack J. Phillips, 10 Steps to Successful Business Alignment, ASTD, ROI Institute, 2012

D-BAM: Diversity Business Alignment Maps

Determining the Payoff Needs

The first step in up-front analysis is to determine the potential payoff of solving a problem or seizing an opportunity. This step begins with answers to a few crucial questions: Is this program or initiative worth doing? Is it feasible? What is the likelihood of a positive ROI? For programs addressing significant problems or opportunities with high potential rewards, the answers are obvious. The questions may take longer to answer for lower-profile programs or those for which the expected payoff is less apparent.

In any case, these are legitimate questions, and the analysis can be as simple or as comprehensive as required. Essentially, a program will pay off in profit increases or in cost savings. Profit increases are generated by programs that drive revenue— for example, those that utilize diverse work teams and/or cultural competency knowledge and skills to improve sales, drive market share, introduce new products, open new markets, enhance customer service, or increase customer loyalty. Other revenue-generating measures include increasing membership, increasing donations, obtaining grants, and generating tuition from new and returning students— all of which, after subtracting the cost of doing business, should leave a profit. However, most initiatives or programs drive cost savings.

D-BAM: Diversity Business Alignment Maps

Cost savings can come through cost reduction or cost avoidance. Improved quality, reduced cycle time, lowered downtime, reduced employee complaints, lower employee turnover, and minimized delays are all examples of cost savings. Cost-avoidance programs are implemented to reduce risks, avoid problems, or prevent unwanted events. Some Diversity and Inclusion professionals may view cost avoidance as an inappropriate measure to use to determine monetary benefits and calculate ROI.

However, if the assumptions prove correct, an avoided cost (e.g., noncompliance fines) can be more rewarding than reducing an actual cost. Preventing a problem is more cost-effective than waiting for the problem to occur and then having to focus on solving it. Although determining the potential payoff is the first step in the needs-analysis process, it is closely related to the next step, determining the business need, since the potential payoff is often based on a consideration of the business. The payoff depends on two factors: (1) the monetary value derived from the business measure's improvement and (2) the approximate cost of the program. Identifying these monetary values in detail usually yields a more credible forecast of what can be expected from the chosen solution. However, this step may be omitted in situations where the business need must be met regardless of the cost or if it becomes obvious that the proposed Diversity and Inclusion initiative or program has a high payoff.

D-BAM: Diversity Business Alignment Maps

The target level of detail may also hinge on the need to secure program funding. If the potential funding source does not recognize the value of the program compared with the potential costs, more detail may be needed to provide a convincing case for funding. Knowledge of the actual payoff is not necessary if widespread agreement exists that the payoff from the program will be high or if the problem in question must be resolved regardless of cost. For example, if the proposed program involves a safety concern, a regulatory compliance issue, or a competitive matter, a detailed analysis is not needed.

The Hubbard Diversity ROI (DROI®) Business Alignment Matrix highlights a sample application of the "V" model to address the high cost of diverse employee turnover and the need to improve retention. After conducting a Business Needs and Performer Needs Analysis, the organization has determined that the costs associated with employee turnover must be addressed and the payoff would be worth it.

D-BAM: Diversity Business Alignment Maps

Level	Needs Assessment	Program Objective	Measurement and Evaluation Approach
7/0	**Business Needs and Performer Needs Analysis** Identify Situation-Problem-Impact- Need-Resolution (SPIN-R)	**HH DROI Phase: Know What You Want to Know** Identify Business Problems/Opportunities Formulate Research Questions Create Diversity Measurement Study Objectives	**Communicate Impact: Output, Outcome, and Results** Demonstrate Organizational Impact in Financial Terms
6	Intangibles Analysis (SOS)		Report Non-Financial Outcomes (Intangibles)
5	**Payoff Needs ->** Avoid Cost Associated with Employee Turnover	**DROI Objectives ->** Targeted Return on Investment of 25%	**DROI** Calculate DROI %
4	**Business Needs ->** Reduce Controllable Turnover Increase Employee Engagement and Satisfaction	**Business Impact Objectives ->** Monthly Percentage of Controllable Employee Turnover Decline Increase Employee Engagement and Satisfaction	**Impact Analysis** Percentage of Controllable Turnover at 8 Months after completion of the DROI Initiative compared to the same measurements taken before the program Use the Hubbard High Performing Workplace Analysis at 6 Months
3	**Job Performance Needs ->** Immediate Manager Effectiveness in the areas of Leadership, Cultural Competence, Diversity Champion Skills and Developing and Motivating Employees	**Application Objectives ->** Effectively and continuously apply the Turnover Prevention Techniques at work Effectively create and sustain motivational work environments that increase employee engagement	**Application Analysis** Participant self-assessment at 3 months after completion of the program Subordinate employee survey 1 month after completion of the program
2	**Learning Needs ->** Increase success skills of immediate managers in the in the areas of Leadership, Cultural Competence, Diversity Champion Skills and Developing and Motivating Employees	**Learning Objectives - >** Immediate managers learn to effectively apply the five self-coaching skills of self-managing, reflecting, acting consciously, collaborating, and evolving Learn how to foster motivational work environments that increase engagement Learn how to recognize and address an inappropriate comment and/or behavior.	**Learning Analysis** Session content summaries, participant assignments, and skill development journal entries during the program Pre/post self-assessment profile Use the Hubbard High Performing Workplace Analysis with direct reports during the program
1	**Preference Needs ->** Learning that is relevant and important to successful job performance	**Reaction Objectives ->** Program content receives favorable rating of 4 out of 5 in relevance and importance 80% of participants identify planned actions	**Reaction Analysis** Reaction and planned action questionnaires at the end of each session of the program

Copyright © 2012 by Hubbard & Hubbard, Inc All Rights Reserved. Tel. 707-763-8380 Confidential and Proprietary

Hubbard Diversity ROI (DROI®) Business Alignment Matrix

Therefore, one of the "strategic Diversity initiatives which will appear on the D-BAM will specifically focus on "reducing diverse employee turnover and improving their retention." Outcome objectives are set at each of the seven levels (Level-0 to Level-6) and the Diversity and Inclusion initiative is executed according to the Hubbard Diversity Return on Investment Methodology (which begins with Analysis and alignment with the organization's business).

D-BAM: Diversity Business Alignment Maps

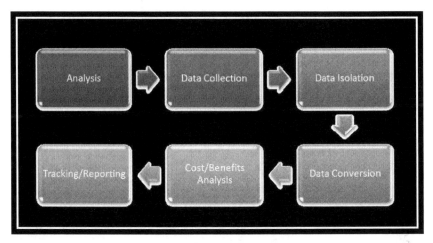

Hubbard Diversity Return on Investment Methodology

Implementing the Diversity and Inclusion initiative according to the Hubbard Diversity ROI (DROI®) Business Alignment Matrix integrates the alignment with the business, beginning with the Business Needs and Performer Needs Analysis and maintains that connection throughout the implementation process to the step requiring calculations to determine the initiative's Diversity Return on Investment (DROI®).

Creating a Strategic Link

Linking and aligning the organization's strategic business objectives with the diversity process is critical to the success of the effort. Diversity and inclusion building processes are not created for their own sake. These processes are built to support, and where appropriate, lead the organization to achieve its vision and strategy. This diversity alignment must be built in concert with the

D-BAM: Diversity Business Alignment Maps

organization's vision and strategy such that the top and bottom of the organization recognizes its roles, responsibilities, and accountabilities for action. For example, senior management roles, responsibilities, and accountabilities might include the following:

Senior Management' Overall Role, Responsibilities, and Critical Accountabilities that Drive Performance

Senior Management's overall role is to provide Diversity and Inclusion leadership and direction in establishing an environment where the full potential of all employees can be utilized, in support of organizational objectives, without regard to ethnic, gender, racial, and other characteristics.

Principal Responsibilities and Activities

Establishing Vision and Strategies

- Include Diversity and Inclusion commentary as part of the organization's mission and strategy statements.
- Co-create the Diversity Business Alignment Map (D-BAM) and Diversity Scorecard to cascade its application to all business units.
- Be clear in articulating what needs to be changed; don't be a guardian of the status quo.
- Develop a sound business rationale for allocating resources to Diversity and Inclusion initiatives,

D-BAM: Diversity Business Alignment Maps

identifying with clarity the potential adverse consequences of inaction.

- Provide for linkage of Diversity and Inclusion activities with other ongoing initiatives in the organization, such as market share improvement, restructuring, leadership development, operational process improvement, etc.

Allocating Resources

- Allocate sufficient budgets to sustain needed activities during both good and weak years of fiscal performance.
- Provide for the appropriate staffing to move the Diversity and Inclusion process forward to implemented programs.
- Appoint senior executives to participate in task forces and other high visibility activities.

Establishing Accountability

- Work with senior managers to establish challenging but realistic goals for Diversity and inclusion interventions and measurable results using the Diversity Business Alignment Map and the Diversity Scorecard.
- Monitor the progress against objectives and include information on results in operational reports.
- Provide appropriate financial or non-financial recognition of Diversity and Inclusion progress, or withhold recognition and rewards when progress is disappointing.

D-BAM: Diversity Business Alignment Maps

Modeling Diversity and Inclusion Leadership Behavior

- Participate in Diversity and Inclusion education and planning.
- Complete a self-assessment of personal biases and preferences that might impede effectiveness in leading the Diversity and Inclusion process.
- Demonstrate a firm commitment in the face of backlash that might be stirred up by the Diversity and Inclusion process.
- Avoid becoming personally defensive about feedback identifying current problems, focusing energies instead on developing solutions.

Putting Principles into Practice

- Implement the Diversity Business Alignment Map (D-BAM) and the Diversity Scorecard perspective initiatives and work to integrate their use in the organization's business processes.
- Create diverse work teams to address meaningful issues.
- Question homogeneity in any organizational activity or at any level of the organization.
- Set policy against organization-sponsored memberships for executives in discriminatory clubs.

D-BAM: Diversity Business Alignment Maps

- Reinforce the Diversity and Inclusion message in communications of all types, making it a normal part of doing business.
- Incorporate Diversity into succession planning processes.
- Develop a personal understanding of the issues, through reading, training and contacts; use the knowledge to support changes in culture, systems and policies.

These are just a few examples of the roles, responsibilities and accountabilities that should be in place to forge organizational alignment.

Implementing the organization's vision and strategy begins with educating and involving the people who must execute it. Some organizations hold their strategy secret, shared only among the senior executive group. The group implements the strategy through central command and control. While this approach was widely used by senior executives for much of the twentieth century, most executives of today's global, technology- and customer-driven organizations realize that they cannot determine and communicate all the local actions required to implement a successful strategy. Organizations that wish to have every employee contribute to the implementation of the business strategy must share their long-term vision and strategy-embodied in the business unit's organizational and Diversity Scorecards, and the D-BAM-with their employees. They must actively encourage them to suggest ways by which the

D-BAM: Diversity Business Alignment Maps

vision and strategy can be achieved. Such feedback and advice engages employees in the future of the organization, and encourages them to be part of the formulation and implementation of its strategy.

In an ideal world, every person in the organization, from the boardroom to the back room, would understand the Diversity and Inclusion strategy and how his or her individual actions support the "big picture." The D-BAM and Diversity Scorecard create this top-to-bottom alignment. The development of the D-BAM and the Diversity Scorecard should begin with the executive team and the Chief Diversity Officer as part of that team.

Executive team building and commitment are an essential part of gaining benefits from the D-BAM and Diversity Scorecard development process. But, they are only the first step. To gain maximum benefit, the executive team should share its vision and strategy for Diversity and Inclusion with the whole organization, as well as with key outside constituents. By communicating the strategy and by linking it to personal goals, the D-BAM and Diversity scorecard creates a shared understanding and commitment among all organizational participants.

When everyone understands the business unit's long-term goals involving and integrating Diversity and Inclusion, as well as the strategy for achieving these goals, all organizational efforts and

D-BAM: Diversity Business Alignment Maps

initiatives can become aligned with the needed transformation processes. Individuals can see how their particular actions contribute to achieving business unit objectives.

The alignment of an organization to a shared Diversity and Inclusion vision (and common direction) is an extended and complex process. Some organizations have eventually involved large numbers of their employees in the alignment process. No single program or event can align this many people. Instead, these large organizations use several interrelated mechanisms to translate the strategy, the D-BAM and the Diversity Scorecard into local objectives and measures that will influence personal and team priorities. Kaplan and Norton cite three distinct mechanisms that can be used.

Communication and Education Programs

A prerequisite for implementing strategy is that all employees, senior corporate executives, and the board of directors understand the Diversity and Inclusion strategy and the required behavior to achieve the strategic business objectives. A consistent and continuing program to educate the organization on the components of the strategy, as well as reinforcing this education with feedback on actual performance, is the foundation of organizational alignment.

D-BAM: Diversity Business Alignment Maps

Goal-Setting Programs

Once a base level of understanding exists, individuals and teams throughout the business unit must translate the higher-level strategic Diversity and Inclusion objectives into personal and team objectives. The traditional management-by-objectives (MBO) programs used by most organizations should be linked to the objectives and measures articulated in the D-BAM and the Diversity Scorecard.

Reward System Linkage

Alignment of the organization toward the Diversity and Inclusion strategy must ultimately be motivated through the incentive and reward systems. While this linkage should be approached carefully, and only after the education and communication programs are in place, many organizations are already benefiting from linking incentive compensation systems to their D-BAM and Diversity Scorecards. Typical objectives for linking the diversity strategy to incentives include:

- Motivating outstanding performance to achieve the strategic, financial, Diversity and Inclusion climate, and operational goals of the organization.
- Provide key managers an opportunity to directly share in the benefits of outstanding Diversity and Inclusion climate, operating and financial performance.

D-BAM: Diversity Business Alignment Maps

- Provide focus on particular areas of organizational concern and reward performance in those areas.

Strategic alignment of an organization and its business unit must take place in multiple directions. The obvious need is to achieve downward alignment to the employee base. This process, frequently referred to as "cascading," is the most complex because of the sheer numbers and logistics involved. Frequently overlooked is the need for upward alignment, to corporate boards and shareholders. Both types of alignment are critical.

Communication and Education Programs

Communication to employees about an organization's Diversity and Inclusion vision and D-BAM strategy should be viewed as an internal marketing campaign. The goals of such a campaign are identical to those of traditional marketing campaigns: to create awareness and to affect behavior. The communication of the D-BAM and Diversity Scorecard should increase each individual's understanding of the organization's Diversity and Inclusion strategy and enhance motivation for acting to achieve strategic Diversity and Inclusion objectives.

A business unit implementing and integrating the processes incorporated in the D-BAM and Diversity Scorecard can have thousands of employees. A communication program to this many people requires a sustained, comprehensive plan. Some

D-BAM: Diversity Business Alignment Maps

organizations, however, treat the D-BAM and Diversity Scorecard as a one-time event. Having just spent several months developing the D-BAM and scorecard and obtaining a shared consensus among the senior management group, they rush to share their new insight with all their employees. But they never follow up the initial publicity splash, and the employees treat the announcement as just another program-of-the-month that can be safely shelved and eventually ignored.

The organizational communication and education program should not only be comprehensive but also periodic. Multiple communication devices can be used to launch the D-BAM and Diversity Scorecard initiatives: executive announcements, videos, town hall meetings, brochures, and newsletters. These initial announcements should then be followed up continually, by reporting D-BAM and scorecard measures and outcomes on bulletin boards, newsletters, groupware, and electronic networks.

There are a number of vehicles that can be used to communicate the organization's Diversity and Inclusion vision and strategies. Using an online brochure, for example, instead of a statement of broad, general themes, the online brochure can describe the specific measures the executives will use to monitor the success of their strategy. The brochure should be updated periodically to report trends and current performance along each of the specific goals, and to describe the initiatives the organization is using to

D-BAM: Diversity Business Alignment Maps

accomplish its goals. Using an online version makes this task easier. In general, organizations are encouraged to communicate the objectives, measures, and targets embodied in the unit's Diversity Scorecard by connecting people with these brochures both in hard copy and online versions throughout the organization to reach a variety of learning styles.

Many organizations use organizational newsletters to embed the D-BAM and Diversity Scorecard in their ongoing communication programs with employees. The newsletter may begin by devoting a section of each monthly newsletter to the D-BAM and Diversity scorecard information. Initially, this section would be used to educate and motivate employees. After communicating the purpose and content of the D-BAM and scorecard in the first few issues, the section can be shifted from education to feedback. Each issue could report recent results on the measures for one perspective. Raw numbers and trends could be supplemented with stories on how a department or an individual was contributing to the reported performance. The vignettes would communicate to the workforce how individuals and teams were using local Diversity and Inclusion initiatives to help the organization implement its business and diversity strategies.

Some organizations, however, have deliberately chosen not to communicate the Diversity Scorecard, for example, to their employees. These organizations feel that their employees have

D-BAM: Diversity Business Alignment Maps

been bombarded, in recent times, with all manner of vision and change programs, and that the employees have become cynical and insulated to high-level pronouncements about the latest management focus that is sure to swiftly transform the organization to breakthrough performance. In order to overcome individual resistance to these types of programs, the Diversity and Inclusion implementation team will use the newsletters to disseminate the broad themes of the D-BAM and Diversity scorecard without specifically labeling or naming this new organizational initiative. That is, executives and the implementation team, for example will talk about the attributes that the organization wishes to deliver to key ethnic customers, but do not label them as the "value propositions for targeted customers." Having stressed the importance of satisfying specific preferences of customers in key ethnic markets, the communication program then emphasizes the processes and metrics that are most important for the organization to excel.

Electronic networks and groupware, like Hubbard & Hubbard, Inc.'s Metriclink system (online or enterprise version), provide additional opportunities for organizations to communicate and gain commitment to the D-BAM and Diversity Scorecard objectives. Organizations can post a complete set of Diversity scorecard objectives and measures using Metriclink's electronic metrics relationship tree and provide key strategies, tactics and action plans

D-BAM: Diversity Business Alignment Maps

in its strategic planning sub-system. Using other media, the Diversity Scorecard presentation can be enhanced to create a comprehensive communications package. With Metriclink, actual results and trends of past performance on each Diversity Scorecard measure can be updated and displayed monthly, quarterly, semi-annually, etc. To be effective, all of these tools must be woven together into a comprehensive communication effort that is directed at achieving strategic alignment over the long term.

The design of such a program should begin by answering several fundamental questions.

- What are the objectives of the communication strategy?
- Who are the target audiences?
- What is the key message for each audience?
- What are the appropriate media for each audience?
- What is the time frame for each stage of the communication strategy?
- How will we know that the communication has been received?

Communicating With the Board of Directors and External Shareholders

The D-BAM and Diversity Scorecard should be communicated upward in an organization to the top, and the organization's board of directors or top-level governance body (if it exist). Conventional

D-BAM: Diversity Business Alignment Maps

rhetoric declares that a principal responsibility of the board or top-level governance body is to provide oversight of organizational, agency, and/or business unit strategy. In practice, however, organizational boards spend more time reviewing and analyzing quarterly financial results than engaging in detailed strategic reviews and analysis. When the primary communication between senior executives and its outside board of directors consists of short-term financial measures, it is not surprising that meetings focus more on short-term operational results than long-term strategic vision. Several experts argue that boards of directors must play a more active role in monitoring organizational strategy and corporate performance, which includes "Diversity and Inclusion performance".

The D-BAM and Diversity Scorecard can and should be the mechanism by which senior executives present their organizational and business unit Diversity and Inclusion strategies to the board of directors. This communication not only informs the board in specific terms that long-term Diversity and Inclusion strategies designed for competitive success are in place, it also provides the basis for feedback and accountability to the board.

Reward Systems Linkage

A major question that is faced by all organizations is whether and how to link their formal compensation system to the Diversity

D-BAM: Diversity Business Alignment Maps

Scorecard measures. Currently, organizations are following different strategies in how soon they link their compensation system to Diversity measures. Ultimately, for the D-BAM and the Diversity Scorecard to drive cultural change, incentive compensation must be connected to achievement of Diversity scorecard objectives. The issue is not whether, but when and how the connection should be made.

Because financial compensation is such a powerful lever, some organizations want to tie their compensation policy for senior managers to the Diversity Scorecard measures as soon as possible.

As seen in the exhibit below, some organizations use an incentive system for Diversity and Inclusion that supports its evolution from activity-based measures in its scorecard to results-based measures:

Year	Activity-Based Measures	Results-Based Measures
Bonus Percentages by Period:	Requires managers to attend courses on diversity and to be active in diverse and/or multi-cultural workforce activities and events. **Requirements:**	Involves meeting the qualitative and quantitative metrics, ratios, and goals for hiring rates, training, promotion, succession planning, ethnic market share and process improvement, innovation,

Page
167

D-BAM: Diversity Business Alignment Maps

		etc. Requirements:
Year 1	100% of Bonus Percentage	0% of Bonus Percentage
Year 2	75%	25%
Year 3	50%	50%
Year 4	25%	75%
Year 5	0%	100%

Note: This accountability system is developmental. Rewards can be given through informal or formal channels (depending on the culture), resulting in higher visibility and more incentives for those who participate actively in the diversity process and achieve its scorecard target objectives.

Source: "Measuring Diversity Results" by Dr. Edward E. Hubbard, Global Insights Publishing, Petaluma, CA, 1997.

This transitional model illustrates how an executive, supervisory, and management accountability system can be created to transition the organization toward performance and incentive-based Diversity and Inclusion metrics focused on results. It shows that as time passes, executives, managers, and supervisors gain increasing responsibility for Diversity and Inclusion results and outcomes rather than simply completing Diversity and Inclusion activities.

This should not suggest that organizations focus only on results. It is also important to examine the process by which the results are attained. Activity-based and process-based measures help build awareness and strategies to accomplish Diversity and Inclusion goals while the scorecard's results-based measures lay the

D-BAM: Diversity Business Alignment Maps

foundation for accepting responsibility for performance. This process helps generate the guidelines for rewards and incentives.

One CEO expressed his pleasure with the results from this plan: "Our organization is aligned with its strategy. I know of no competitor that has this degree of alignment. It is producing results for us." Obviously, tying incentive compensation to your Diversity scorecard measures is attractive, but it has some risks. Are the right measures on the scorecard? Are the data for the selected measures reliable? Could there be unintended or unexpected consequences in how the targets for the measures are achieved? The disadvantages occur when the initial Diversity Scorecard measures are not perfect surrogates for the strategic objectives, and when the actions that improve the short-term measured results may be inconsistent with achieving the long-term objectives. This highlights the importance of having a Diversity and Inclusion measurement professional available to help the implementation team make key metric selections to include in the scorecard. Obtaining specialized professional Diversity and Inclusion measurement resources are available through Hubbard & Hubbard, Inc. and the Hubbard Diversity ROI Institute. We can assist in developing and implementing these strategic processes.

In several organizations, the clear articulation in a Diversity Scorecard of business unit strategic Diversity and Inclusion objectives, with links to associated performance drivers, has

D-BAM: Diversity Business Alignment Maps

enabled many individuals to see, often for the first time, the links between what they do and the organization's long-term business objectives. Rather than behaving on automatic pilot, with bonuses tied to achieving or exceeding targets in the performance of their local tasks without regard to their Diversity and Inclusion implications, individuals can now identify the tasks they should be doing exceptionally well to help achieve the organization's Diversity and Inclusion as well as and other key objectives. This articulation of the D-BAM and how individual tasks align with overall business unit objectives creates intrinsic motivation among employees. Their innovation and problem-solving energies can become unleashed, even without explicit ties to compensation incentives. Of course, since extrinsic motivation remains important, and if the organization begins to achieve breakthrough performance by meeting or exceeding the stretch targets for its strategic Diversity and Inclusion measures, the employees who made such performance happen should be recognized and rewarded. Experimenting and monitoring changes will provide additional evidence on the appropriate balance between explicit, objective formulas and subjective evaluation for linking incentive compensation to achievement of Diversity Scorecard objectives.

Final Thoughts

Utilizing the D-BAM and formulating a Diversity Scorecard that links a business unit's mission and strategy to explicit Diversity

D-BAM: Diversity Business Alignment Maps

and Inclusion objectives (and measures) is only the start of using the D-BAM and Diversity Scorecard as a comprehensive management system. The D-BAM and the Diversity Scorecard must be communicated to a variety of organizational constituents, especially employees, corporate-level managers, and boards of directors. The goal of the communication process is to align all employees within the organization, as well as individuals to whom the business unit is accountable (corporate executives and the board), to the Diversity and business strategy. The knowledge and alignment among these constituents will facilitate local goal setting, feedback, and accountability to the SBU's strategic path in utilizing Diversity and Inclusion.

Alignment and accountability will clearly be enhanced when individual contributions to achieving the D-BAM and Diversity Scorecard objectives are linked to recognition, promotion, and compensation programs. It sends the appropriate message that utilization of diverse human and other resources is in alignment with exceptional business excellence and performance!

References

Kaplan, Robert S.; Norton, David P.. Strategy Maps: Converting Intangible Assets into Tangible Outcomes (Kindle Locations 3205-3206). Harvard Business Review Press. Kindle Edition.

D-BAM: Diversity Business Alignment Maps

Kaplan, Robert S.; Norton, David P.. Strategy Maps: Converting Intangible Assets into Tangible Outcomes (Kindle Locations 3202-3205). Harvard Business Review Press. Kindle Edition.

Kaplan, Robert S.; Norton, David P.. Strategy Maps: Converting Intangible Assets into Tangible Outcomes (Kindle Locations 3213-3214). Harvard Business Review Press. Kindle Edition.

Kaplan, Robert S.; Norton, David P.. Strategy Maps: Converting Intangible Assets into Tangible Outcomes (Kindle Locations 3214-3220). Harvard Business Review Press. Kindle Edition.

Kaplan, Robert S.; Norton, David P.. Strategy Maps: Converting Intangible Assets into Tangible Outcomes (Kindle Locations 3261-3262). Harvard Business Review Press. Kindle Edition.

"Unleashing the Strategic Power of Diversity ROI Measurement", Hubbard, Edward E., Diversity Executive Magazine, November 17, 2013

Kaplan, Robert S.; Norton, David P.. Strategy Maps: Converting Intangible Assets into Tangible Outcomes (Kindle Locations 3198-3201). Harvard Business Review Press. Kindle Edition.

Phillips, Jack; Phillips, Patricia Pulliam. High-Impact Human Capital Strategy: Addressing the 12 Major Challenges Today's Organizations Face (Kindle Locations 1435-1437). AMACOM. Kindle Edition.

Phillips, Jack; Phillips, Patricia Pulliam. High-Impact Human Capital Strategy: Addressing the 12 Major Challenges Today's Organizations Face (Kindle Locations 1457-1460). AMACOM. Kindle Edition.

Phillips, Jack; Phillips, Patricia Pulliam. High-Impact Human Capital Strategy: Addressing the 12 Major Challenges Today's

D-BAM: Diversity Business Alignment Maps

Organizations Face (Kindle Locations 1478-1480). AMACOM. Kindle Edition.

Phillips, Jack; Phillips, Patricia Pulliam. *High-Impact Human Capital Strategy: Addressing the 12 Major Challenges Today's Organizations Face* (Kindle Locations 1483-1484). AMACOM. Kindle Edition.

Baytos, Lawrence M. *Designing & Implementing Successful Diversity Programs.* New Jersey: Prentice Hall, 1995.

Becker, Brian E., Huselid, Mark A., and Ulrich, Dave. *The HR Scorecard: Linking People, Strategy, and Performance.* Boston: Harvard Business School Press, 2001.

Brown, Mark Graham, "Keeping Score", Quality Resources, New York, NY, 1996.

Brown, Mark Graham, "Winning Score", Productivity, Inc., Portland, OR, 2000.

Hubbard, Edward E., "Measuring Diversity Results", Global Insights Publishing, Petaluma, CA, 1997.

Kaplan, Robert S., and Norton, David P., *The Balanced Scorecard,* Harvard Business School Press, Boston, MA, 1996.

Further Readings

Daniels, Aubrey. *Bringing Out the Best in People-How to Apply the Astonishing Power of Positive Reinforcement.* New York: McGraw-Hill, 1994.

Drucker, Peter F. "The Information Executives Truly Need." *Harvard Business Review,* January/February 1995.

D-BAM: Diversity Business Alignment Maps

Eccles, Robert G. "The Performance Measurement Manifesto." *Harvard Business Review,* January/February 1991.

Hubbard, Edward E., "The Diversity Scorecard Fieldbook", Global Insights Publishing, Petaluma, CA, 2003.

Hubbard, Edward E., "How to Calculate Diversity Return on Investment", Global Insights Publishing, Petaluma, CA, 1999.

Chapter Six: Creating the Strategy-focused Diversity Organization

A study of 275 portfolio managers reported that the ability to execute strategy was more important than the quality of the strategy itself. These managers cited strategy implementation as the most important factor shaping management and corporate valuations. This finding seems surprising since the past two decades highlighted many management theorists, consultants, and the business press heavily focused the reader's attention on how to gain skills to devise strategies that will generate superior performance. Apparently, strategy formulation has never been more important. Yet other observers concur with the portfolio managers' opinion that the ability to **_execute_** strategy can be **more important** than the strategy itself. It is estimated that 70 percent of the lack of strategic performance by organizations is due to the failure to execute strategy. With organization failure rates reported in the 70 percent to 90 percent range, we can appreciate why sophisticated investors have come to realize that **execution** is more important than good vision.

Why do organizations have difficulty implementing well-formulated strategies? One problem is that strategies—the unique

D-BAM: Diversity Business Alignment Maps

and sustainable ways by which organizations create value—are changing but the tools for measuring strategies have not kept pace. In the industrial economy, companies created value with their tangible assets, by transforming raw materials into finished products. A 1982 Brookings Institute study showed that tangible book values represented 62 percent of industrial organizations' market values. Ten years later, the ratio had dropped to 38 percent. And recent studies estimated that the book value of tangible assets accounts for only 10 percent to 15 percent of companies' market values.

Clearly, opportunities for creating value are shifting from managing tangible assets to managing knowledge-based strategies that deploy an organization's intangible assets: customer relationships, innovative products and services, high-quality and responsive operating processes, information technology and databases, and employee capabilities, skills, and motivation. In an economy dominated by tangible assets, financial measurements were adequate to record investments in inventory, property, plant, and equipment on companies' balance sheets. Income statements could also capture the expenses associated with the use of these tangible assets to produce revenues and profits. But in today's economy, where intangible assets have become the major sources of competitive advantage, indicate a need for tools that describe knowledge-based assets and the value-creating strategies that these

D-BAM: Diversity Business Alignment Maps

assets make possible. This same observation is true looking through the lens of Diversity and Inclusion. Tools have not kept pace assisting Diversity and Inclusion professionals with the need to show measurable evidence that Diversity and Inclusion strategies are important in driving organizational strategies for success. This is one of the reasons I developed the D-BAM tool and process.

Lacking such tools, companies have and will continue to encounter difficulties managing what they cannot not describe or measure. Companies also have had problems attempting to implement knowledge-based strategies in organizations designed for industrial-age competition. Many organizations, even until the end of the 1970s, operated under central control, through large functional departments. This allowed organizational strategy to be developed at the top and implemented through a centralized command-and-control culture. As a result, change was incremental. Managers used slow-reacting and tactical management control systems such as the budget to assess progress and impact. Such systems, however, were designed for nineteenth- and early twentieth-century industrial companies and are inadequate for today's dynamic, rapidly changing environment. Yet many organizations continue to use them. Is it any surprise that they have difficulty implementing radical new strategies that were

D-BAM: Diversity Business Alignment Maps

designed for knowledge-based competition in the twenty-first century?

Organizations need a new kind of management system, like D-BAMs, to manage diverse human capital—one explicitly designed to manage strategy, not tactics. Most of today's organizations operate through decentralized business units and teams that are much closer to the customer than large corporate staffs. These organizations recognize that competitive advantage comes more from the intangible knowledge, capabilities, and relationships created by employees than from investments in physical assets and access to capital. Strategy implementation therefore requires that all business units, support units, and employees are aligned and linked to the organization's strategy. And with the rapid changes in technology, competition, and regulations, the formulation and implementation of strategy must become a continual and participative process. Organizations today need a language for communicating strategy as well as processes and systems that help them to implement strategy and gain feedback about their strategy. Success comes from strategy when its implementation becomes everyone's job.

D-BAM: Diversity Business Alignment Maps

Building a Strategy-Supportive Corporate Culture

Every organization is a unique culture. It has its own history, its own ways of approaching problems and conducting activities, its own mix of managerial personalities and styles, its own patterns of "how we do things around here," its own set of war stories and heroes, its own experiences of how changes have been instituted-in other words, its own atmosphere, folklore, and personality. A company's culture can be weak and fragmented in the sense that most people have no heartfelt sense of company purpose, view their jobs as simply a way to make money, and have divided loyalties-some to their department, some to their colleagues, some to the union, and some to their boss. On the other hand, a company's culture can be strong and cohesive in the sense that most people understand the company's objectives and strategy, know what their individual roles are, and work conscientiously to do their part. A strong culture is a powerful lever for channeling behavior and helping employees do their jobs in a more strategy-supportive manner; this occurs in two ways:

- By knowing exactly what is expected of them, employees in strong- culture firms don't have to waste time figuring out what to do or how to do it-the culture provides a system of informal rules and peer pressures regarding how to behave most of the time. In a weak-culture

D-BAM: Diversity Business Alignment Maps

company, the absence of strong company identity and a purposeful work climate results in substantial employee confusion and wasted effort.

- A strong culture turns a job into a way of life; it provides structure, standards, and a value system in which to operate; and it promotes strong company identification among employees. As a result, employees feel better about what they do, and more often than not, they work harder to help the company become more successful.

This says something important about the leadership task of strategy implementation: to implement and execute a strategic plan, an organization's culture must be closely aligned with its strategy.

The optimal condition is a work environment so in tune with strategy that strategy-critical activities are performed in superior fashion. As one observer of Toyota noted:

"It has not been just strategy that led to big Japanese wins in the American auto market. It is a culture that motivates workers to excel at fits and finishes, to produce moldings that match and doors that don't sag. It is a culture in which Toyota can use that most sophisticated of management tools, the suggestion box, and in two years increase the number of worker suggestions from under 10,000 to over 1 million with resultant savings of $250 million."

D-BAM: Diversity Business Alignment Maps

What Is Organizational and Corporate Culture?

Organizational culture is "the set of shared, taken-for-granted implicit assumptions that a group holds and that determines how it perceives, thinks about, and reacts to its various environments" (Schein, 1996). This definition highlights two important characteristics of organizational culture. First, organizational culture influences our behavior at work. The second key characteristic of organizational culture is that it operates on two levels, which vary in terms of outward visibility and resistance to change.

At the less visible level, culture reflects the values shared among organizational members. At the more visible level, culture represents the normative behavior patterns accepted by organizational members. These patterns are passed on to others through the socialization process. Culture is more susceptible to change at this level. Each level of culture influences the other. For example, if an organization truly values providing high-quality service to ethnic markets, employees are more likely to adopt the behavior of responding faster to emerging market customer complaints. The D-BAM leverages these characteristics by structuring Diversity and Inclusion initiatives which focus on aligning the work behavior of a diverse workforce to drive critical objectives and outcomes reflected in the organization's strategic business plan and Mission.

D-BAM: Diversity Business Alignment Maps

The taproot of **_corporate culture_** is the organization's beliefs and philosophy about how its affairs ought to be conducted. It reveals the reasons why it does things the way it does. A company's philosophy and beliefs can be hard to pin down, even harder to characterize. In a sense they are intangible. They are manifest in the values and business principles that senior managers espouse, in the ethical standards they demand, in the policies they set, in the style with which things are done, in the traditions the organization maintains, in people's attitudes and feelings and in the stories they tell, in the peer pressures that exist, in the organization's politics, and in the "chemistry" that surrounds the work environment and defines the organization's culture.

Manifestations of Culture

When is an organization's culture most apparent? One theory suggests that cultural assumptions assert themselves through socialization of new employees, subculture clashes, and top management behavior. Consider these three situations:

- **Situation 1:** A newly hired Hispanic employee who shows up late for an important meeting is told a story about someone who was fired for repeated tardiness.
- **Situation 2:** Conflict between product design engineers who emphasize a product's function and marketing

D-BAM: Diversity Business Alignment Maps

specialists who demand a more stylish product reveals an underlying clash of subculture values.

- **Situation 3:** Top managers, through the behavior they model and the administrative and reward systems they create, prompt a significant improvement in the quality of a company's products.

Each of these situations highlights the makings of workplace culture whose impact must be measured to determine its application and effects on diverse groups throughout the organization.

Vijay Sathe, a Harvard Researcher, developed a useful model for observing and interpreting organizational culture (see Model)

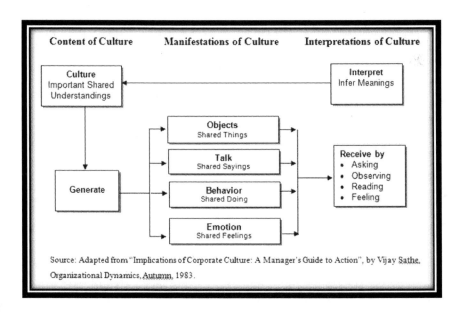

Source: Adapted from "Implications of Corporate Culture: A Manager's Guide to Action", by Vijay Sathe, Organizational Dynamics, Autumn, 1983.

D-BAM: Diversity Business Alignment Maps

This model highlights four general manifestations or evidence of workplace culture that includes shared things (objects), shared sayings (talk), shared doings (behavior), and shared feelings (emotion). To create an effective D-BAM, Diversity practitioners can begin collecting cultural information within the workplace by asking, observing, reading, and feeling (experiencing) the culture.

An organization's culture also fulfils four functions. To help bring these four functions to life, let's consider how each of them has taken shape at the 3M (Jocobs, 1995; Anfuso, 1995). This 3M example is a particularly helpful in understanding these four functions because it has a long history of being an innovative company-the company was founded in 1902. It is consistently ranked as one of the most admired company in the US, partly due to its strong and distinctive culture.

1. *Give members an organizational identity.* 3M is known as being an innovative company that relentlessly pursues new-product development. The organization's top management, for example, decreed that 30 per cent of sales must come from products introduced within the past four years. The old standard was 25 per cent in five years. Creating rewards that reinforce innovation reinforces this identity. For example, "The 3M Corporation has its version of a Nobel Prize for innovative employees. The prize is the Golden Step award, whose trophy is a winged foot. Several Golden

D-BAM: Diversity Business Alignment Maps

Steps are given out each year to employees whose new products have reached significant revenue and profit levels."

2. *Facilitate collective commitment.* One of 3M's corporate values is to be "a company that a diverse workforce is proud to be a part of'. People who like 3M's culture tend to stay employed there for long periods of time. This collective commitment results in a turnover rate of less than 3 per cent among salaried personnel. Consider the commitment and pride expressed by Kathleen Stanislawski, a staffing manager. "I'm a 27-year 3Mer because, quite frankly, there's no reason to leave. I've had great opportunities to do different jobs and to grow a career. It's just a great company."

3. *Promote social system stability.* Social system stability reflects the extent to which the work environment is perceived as positive and reinforcing, and conflict and change are managed effectively. This stability is reinforced within 3M through a "promote-from within" culture, a strategic hiring policy that ensures that a diverse group of capable college graduates are hired in a timely manner, and a layoff policy that provides displaced workers six months to find another job at 3M before being terminated. Executives also attempt to reduce resistance to change by continually communicating the company's quest for new-product development and continuous improvement of internal processes.

4. *Shape behavior by helping members make sense of their surroundings.* This function of culture helps employees understand why the organization does what it does and how it intends to accomplish its long-term goals. 3M sets expectations for innovation in a variety of ways. For example, the company employs an internship and coop-program. Research into 3M's history showed, for instance, 30 per cent of 3M's college hires came through an internship or coop program. 3M also shape expectations and behavior by providing detailed career feedback to its employees. New staff are measured and evaluated against a career growth standard during their first six months to three years of employment.

We are beginning to learn that an organization's culture is an important contributor (or obstacle) to successful strategy execution. A close culture-strategy match is crucial to managing an organization's people resources with maximum effectiveness. A culture that energizes people all over the firm to do their jobs in a strategy-supportive manner adds significantly to the power and effectiveness of strategy execution. When a company's culture and strategy are out of sync, the culture has to be changed as rapidly as possible; a sizable and prolonged strategy-culture conflict weakens and may even defeat managerial efforts to make the strategy work.

D-BAM: Diversity Business Alignment Maps

The list below includes some of the traits and characteristics of strong-culture companies to provide more insight into why the culture-strategy fit makes such a big difference:

- Importance of customers and customer service
- Commitment of quality
- Commitment to innovation
- Respect for the individual employee and the duty the company has to employees
- Importance of honesty, integrity, and ethical standards
- Duty to stockholders
- Duty to suppliers
- Corporate citizenship
- Importance of protecting the environment

While the examples help demonstrate the contribution culture can make toward "keeping the herd moving roughly West" (as Professor Terrence Deal puts it), the strategy-implementer's concern is with what actions to take to create a culture that facilitates strategy execution.

Creating the fit between Strategy and Culture

It is the *strategy-maker's (the Diversity and Inclusion Practitioner)* responsibility to select a Diversity and Inclusion strategy for the D-BAM that is compatible with the "sacred" or unchangeable parts of prevailing corporate culture. It is the *strategy-implementer's (also*

D-BAM: Diversity Business Alignment Maps

the Diversity and Inclusion Practitioner) task, once strategy is chosen, to bring corporate culture into close alignment with the strategy and keep it there.

Aligning culture with strategy presents a strong challenge. The first step is to diagnose which facets of the present culture are strategy-supportive and which are not. Then, there must be some innovative thinking about concrete actions management can take to modify the cultural environment and create a stronger fit with the strategy.

Symbolic Actions and Substantive Actions

Normally, managerial actions to tighten the culture-strategy fit are both symbolic and substantive. Symbolic actions are valuable for the signals they send about the kinds of behavior and performance strategy implementers wish to encourage. The most common symbolic actions are events held to honor new kinds of heroes-people whose actions and performance serve as role models. Many universities give outstanding teacher awards each year to symbolize their commitment to and esteem for instructors who display exceptional classroom talents. Numerous businesses have employee-of-the-month awards. The military has a long- standing custom of awarding ribbons and medals for exemplary actions. Some football coaches award emblems to players to ·wear on their helmets as symbols of their exceptional performance.

D-BAM: Diversity Business Alignment Maps

Successful strategy-implementers are experts in the use of symbols to build and nurture the culture. They personally conduct ceremonial events, and they go out of their way to personally and publicly congratulate individuals who exhibit the desired traits. Individuals and groups that "get with the program" are singled out for special praise and visibly rewarded. Successful implementers use every ceremonial function and every conversation to implant values, send reinforcing signals, and praise good deeds.

In addition to being out front, personally leading the push for new attitudes and communicating the reasons for new approaches, the manager has to convince all those concerned that the effort is more than cosmetic. Talk and symbols have to be complemented by substance and real movement. The actions taken have to be credible, highly visible, and unmistakably indicative of management's commitment to a new culture and new ways of doing business. There are several ways to accomplish this. One is to engineer some quick successes in reorienting the way some things are done to highlight the value of the new order, thus making enthusiasm for the changes contagious. However, instant results are usually not as important as creating a solid, competent team psychologically committed to carrying out the strategy in a superior fashion. The strongest signs that management is committed to creating a new culture come from actions to replace traditional managers with "new breed" managers, changes in

D-BAM: Diversity Business Alignment Maps

long-standing policies and operating practices, major reorganizational moves, big shifts in how raises and promotions are granted, and reallocations in the budget.

At the same time, chief strategy-implementers must be careful to *lead by example*. For instance, if the organization's strategy involves a drive to become the industry's low-cost producer, senior managers must be frugal in their own actions and decisions: Spartan decorations in the executive suite, conservative expense accounts and entertainment allowances, a lean staff in the corporate office, and so on.

Implanting the needed culture-building values and behavior depends on a sincere, sustained commitment by the chief executive coupled with extraordinary persistence in reinforcing the culture through both word and deed. Neither charisma nor personal magnetism is essential. However, being highly visible around the organization is essential; culture-building cannot be done from an office. Moreover, creating and sustaining a strategy-supportive culture is a job for the whole management team. Senior officers have to keynote the values and shape the organization's philosophy. But for the effort to be successful, strategy-implementers; must enlist the support of subordinate managers, getting them to instill values and establish culture norms at the lowest levels in the organization. Until a big majority of employees have joined the culture and share an emotional commitment to its

D-BAM: Diversity Business Alignment Maps

basic values and beliefs, there's considerably more work to be done in both installing the culture and tightening the culture-strategy fit.

The task of making culture supportive of strategy is not a short-term exercise. It takes time for a new culture to emerge and prevail. The bigger the organization and the greater the cultural shift needed to produce a culture- strategy fit, the longer it takes. In large companies, changing the corporate culture in significant ways can take three to five years at minimum. In fact, it is usually tougher to reshape a deeply ingrained culture that is not strategy-supportive than it is to instill a strategy-supportive culture from scratch in a brand new organization.

Building a Spirit of High Performance into the Culture

An ability to instill strong individual commitment to strategic success and create constructive pressure to perform is one of the most valuable strategy implementing skills. When an organization performs consistently at or near peak capability, the outcome is not only improved strategic success but also an organizational culture permeated with a spirit of high performance. This should not be confused with whether employees are" happy" or "satisfied," or "get along well together." An organization with a spirit of performance emphasizes achievement and excellence. Its culture is

D-BAM: Diversity Business Alignment Maps

results-oriented, and its management pursues policies and practices that inspire people to do their best.

Companies with a spirit of high performance typically are intensely people- oriented; and they reinforce this orientation at every conceivable occasion in every conceivable way to every employee. They treat employees with dignity and respect, train each employee thoroughly, encourage employees to use their own initiative and creativity in performing their work, set reasonable and clear performance expectations, utilize the full range of rewards and punishment to enforce high performance standards, hold managers at every level responsible for developing the people who report to them, and grant employees enough autonomy to stand out, excel, and contribute. To create a results oriented organizational culture, a company must make champions out of the people who turn in winning performances:

- At Boeing, IBM, General Electric, and 3M Corporation, top executives deliberately make "champions" out of individuals who believe so strongly in their ideas that they take it on themselves to hurdle the bureaucracy, maneuver their projects through the system, and turn them into improved services, new products, or even new businesses. In these companies, "product champions" are given high visibility, room to push their ideas, and strong executive support. Champions whose ideas prove out are

D-BAM: Diversity Business Alignment Maps

usually handsomely rewarded; those whose ideas don't pan out still have secure jobs and are given chances to try again.

- The manager of a New York area sales office rented New York's Baseball stadium for an evening. After work, the salesmen were all assembled at the stadium and asked to run one at a time through the player's tunnel onto the field. As each one emerged, the electronic scoreboard flashed his name to those gathered in the stands-executives from corporate headquarters, employees from the office, family, and friends. Their role was to cheer loudly in honor of the individual's sales accomplishments. The company involved was IBM. The occasion for this action was to reaffirm IBM's commitment to satisfy an individual's need to be part of something great and to reiterate IBM's concern for championing individual accomplishment.

- Some companies upgrade the importance and status of individual employees by referring to them as Cast members (Disney), Crew Members (McDonald's), or Associates (Wal-Mart and J.C. Penney). Companies like IBM, Tupperware, and McDonald's actively seek out reasons and opportunities to give pins, buttons, badges, and medals to good showings by average performers-the

D-BAM: Diversity Business Alignment Maps

idea being to express appreciation and help give a boost to the "middle 60 percent" of the work force.

- McDonald's has a contest to determine the best hamburger cooker in its entire chain. It begins with a competition to determine the best hamburger cooker in each store. Store winners go on to compete in regional championships, and regional winners go on to the "All-American" contest. The winners get trophies and an All-American patch to wear on their shirts.

- Milliken & Co. holds Corporate Sharing Rallies once every three months; teams come from all over the company to swap success stories and ideas. A hundred or more teams make five-minute presentations over a two-day period. Each rally has a major theme-quality, cost reduction, and so on. No criticisms and negatives are allowed, and there is no such thing as a big idea or a small one. Quantitative measures of success are used to gauge improvement. All those present vote on the best presentation, and several ascending grades of awards are handed out. Everyone, however, receives a framed certificate for participating.

What makes a spirit of high performance come alive is a complex network of practices, words, symbols, styles, values, and policies pulling together to produce extraordinary results with ordinary

D-BAM: Diversity Business Alignment Maps

people. The drivers of the system are a belief in the worth of the individual, strong company commitments to job security and promotion from within, managerial practices that encourage employees to exercise individual initiative and creativity, and pride in doing the "itty-bitty, teeny-tiny things" right. A company that treats its employees well benefits from increased teamwork, higher morale, and greater employee loyalty.

While emphasizing a spirit of high performance nearly always accentuates the positive, there are negative aspects too. Managers whose units consistently perform poorly have to be removed. Aside from the organizational benefits, weak performing managers should be reassigned for their own good. People who find themselves in a job they cannot handle are usually frustrated, anxiety ridden, harassed, and unhappy. Moreover, subordinates have a right to be managed with competence, dedication, and achievement; unless their boss performs well, they themselves cannot perform well. Weak-performing workers and people who reject the cultural emphasis on dedication and high performance have to be weeded out. Recruitment practices need to aim at selecting highly motivated, ambitious applicants whose attitudes and work habits mesh well with a results-oriented culture.

D-BAM: Diversity Business Alignment Maps

Fostering a Strategy-Supportive Climate and Culture

To execute a D-BAM successfully, strategy-implementers have to be "out front" in promoting a strategy-supportive organizational climate which integrates the use of Diversity and Inclusion performance improvement solutions. When major strategic changes are being implemented, a manager's time is best spent personally leading the changes. When only strategic fine-tuning is being implemented, it takes less time and effort to bring values and culture into alignment with strategy, but there is still a lead role for the manager to play in pushing ahead and prodding for continuous improvements. Successful strategy leaders know it is their responsibility to convince people that the chosen strategy is right and that implementing it to the best of the organization's ability is "top priority."

Both words and deeds play a part. Words inspire people, infuse spirit and drive, define strategy-supportive cultural norms and values, articulate the rea- sons for strategic and organizational change, legitimize new viewpoints and new priorities, urge and reinforce commitment, and arouse confidence in the new strategy. Deeds add credibility to the words, create strategy-supportive symbols, set examples, give meaning and content to the language, and teach the organization what sort of behavior is needed and expected. Highly visible symbols and imagery are needed to

D-BAM: Diversity Business Alignment Maps

complement substantive actions. For example, one General Motors manager explained the striking difference in performance between two large plants. At the poorly performing plant, the plant manager probably ventured out on the floor once a week, always in a suit. His comments were distant and perfunctory. At South Gate, the better plant, the plant manager was on the floor all the time. He wore a baseball cap and a UAW jacket.

As a rule, the greater the degree of strategic change being implemented and/or the greater the shift in cultural norms needed to accommodate a new strategy, the more visible the strategy-implementer's words and deeds need to be. Lessons from well-managed companies show that what the strategy-leader says and does has a significant bearing on down-the-line strategy implementation and execution.

According to one view, "It is not so much the articulation about what an organization should be doing that creates new practice. It's the imagery that creates the understanding, the compelling moral necessity that the new way is right." Moreover, the actions and images, both substantive and symbolic, have to be repeated regularly, not just at ceremonies and special occasions. This is where a high profile and "managing by walking around" comes into play. As a Hewlett-Packard official expresses it in the company publication *The HP Way:*

D-BAM: Diversity Business Alignment Maps

"Once a division or department has developed a plan of its own-a set of working objectives-it's important for managers and supervisors to keep it in operating condition. This is where observation, measurement, feedback, and guidance come in. It's our "management by wandering around. (MBWA)" That's how you find out whether you're on-track and heading at the right speed and in the right direction. If you don't constantly monitor how people are operating, not only will they tend to wander off track but also they will begin to believe you weren't serious about the plan in the first place. It has the extra benefit of getting you off your chair and moving around your area. By wandering around, I literally mean moving around and talking to people. It's all done on a very informal and spontaneous basis, but it's important in the course of time to cover the whole territory.

You start out by being accessible and approachable, but the main thing is to realize you're there to listen. The second reason for MBWA is that it is vital to keep people informed about what's going on in the company, especially those things that are important to them. The third reason for doing this is because it is just plain fun.

Such contacts give the manager a feel for how things are progressing, and they provide opportunities to encourage employees, lift spirits, shift attention from the old to the new priorities, create some excitement, and project an atmosphere of

D-BAM: Diversity Business Alignment Maps

informality and fun -- all of which drive D-BAM implementation in a positive fashion and intensify the organizational energy behind strategy execution.

Jack Welch, formerly with General Electric, sums up the hands-on role and motivational approach well: "I was there every day, or out into a factory, smelling it, feeling it, touching it, and challenging the people."

Keeping the Internal Organization Responsive and Innovative

While formulating and implementing strategy is a manager's responsibility, the task of generating fresh ideas, identifying new opportunities, and responding to changing conditions cannot be accomplished by a single person. It is an organization-wide task, particularly in large corporations. Strategic leadership must result in a dependable supply of fresh ideas from the rank and file-managers and employees alike-and promote an entrepreneurial, opportunistic spirit that permits continuous adaptation to changing conditions. A flexible, responsive, innovative internal environment is critical in fast-moving high- technology industries, in businesses where products have short life cycles and growth depends on new-product innovation, in corporations with widely diversified business portfolios (where opportunities are varied and scattered), in industries where successful product differentiation is key, and in

D-BAM: Diversity Business Alignment Maps

businesses where the strategy of being the low-cost producer hinges on productivity improvement and cost reduction. Managers cannot mandate such an environment by simply telling people to be "creative."

One useful leadership approach is to take special pains to foster, nourish, and support people who are willing to champion new ideas, better services, new products and product applications, and who are eager for a chance to turn their ideas into new divisions, new businesses, and even new industries. When Texas Instruments reviewed some 50 or so successful and unsuccessful new- product introductions, one factor marked every failure: "Without exception it was revealed that each initiative didn't have a volunteer champion. They had someone they had cajoled into taking on the task. Now, when they take a look at a product and decide whether to push it or not, they make certain they've got a new set of criteria. Number one is the presence of a zealous, volunteer champion. After that comes market potential and project economics as a distant second and third." The rule seems to be an idea for something new or something different must either find a champion or die. And the champion needs to be someone who is persistent, competitive, tenacious, committed, and fanatic about the idea and seeing it through to success.

D-BAM: Diversity Business Alignment Maps

Fostering Champions

In order to promote an organizational climate where champions can blossom and thrive, strategy managers need to do several things. First, individuals and groups have to be encouraged to bring their ideas forward, be creative, and exercise initiative. Second, the champion's maverick style has to be tolerated and given room to operate. People's imaginations need to be encouraged to "fly in all directions." Freedom to experiment and informal brainstorming sessions need to become ingrained. Above all, employees from diverse backgrounds and experiences with "out-of-the-box" creative ideas must not be looked on as disruptive or troublesome. Third, managers have to induce and promote lots of attempts and be willing to tolerate mistakes and failures. Most ideas don't pan out, but people learn from a good attempt even when it fails. Fourth, strategy managers should use all kinds of ad hoc organizational forms to support ideas and experimentation such as "venture teams", task forces, internal competition among different groups working on the same project (IBM calls the showdown between the competing approaches a "performance shootout"), informal "bootlegged" projects composed of volunteers, and so on. Fifth, strategy managers have to ensure that rewards for a successful champion are large and visible and that people who champion an unsuccessful idea are encouraged to try again rather

D-BAM: Diversity Business Alignment Maps

than punished or shunted aside. In effect, the leadership task here is to devise internal support systems for entrepreneurial innovation.

Dealing with Company Politics

A manager can't formulate and implement strategy effectively without being perceptive about company politics and adept at political maneuvering. Politics virtually always comes into play in formulating the strategic plan. Inevitably, key individuals and groups form coalitions, and each group presses the benefits and potential of its own ideas and vested interests. Politics can influence which objectives take precedence and which businesses in the portfolio have priority in resource allocation. Internal politics is a factor in building a consensus for one strategic option over another.

As a rule, politics has even more influence in strategy implementation. Typically, internal political considerations affect organization structure (whose areas of responsibility need to be reorganized, who reports to who, who has how much authority over subunits), staffing decisions (what individuals should fill key positions and head strategy-critical activities), and budget allocations (which organizational units will get the biggest increases). .

In short, political considerations and the forming of individual and group alliances are integral parts of building organization-wide

D-BAM: Diversity Business Alignment Maps

support for the strategic plan and gaining consensus on how to implement it. Political skills are a definite requirement, maybe even necessary, asset for managers in orchestrating the whole strategic process.

A strategy manager must understand how an organization's power structure works, who wields influence in the executive ranks, which groups and individuals are "activists" and which are "defenders of the status quo," who can be helpful in a showdown on key decisions, and which direction the political winds are blowing on a given issue. When major decisions have to be made, strategy managers need to be especially sensitive to the politics of managing coalitions and reaching consensus. As a senior executive of a British corporation expressed it:

"I've never taken a major decision without consulting my colleagues. It would be unimaginable to me, unimaginable. First, they help me make a better decision in most cases. Second, if they know about it and agree with it, they'll back it. Otherwise, they might challenge it, not openly, but subconsciously."

The "politics of strategy building and execution" centers chiefly around generating options, nurturing support for strong proposals and killing the weak ones. It also includes guiding the formation of coalitions on particular issues, and achieving consensus and commitment. A recent study of strategy management in nine large

D-BAM: Diversity Business Alignment Maps

corporations showed that successful executives used the following political tactics:

- Letting weakly supported ideas and proposals die through inaction.
- Establishing additional hurdles or tests for strongly supported ideas that the manager views as unacceptable but that are best not opposed openly.
- Keeping a low political profile on unacceptable proposals by getting subordinate managers to say no.
- Letting most negative decisions come from a group consensus that the manager merely confirms, thereby reserving personal veto for big issues and crucial moments.
- Leading the strategy but not dictating it-giving few orders, announcing few decisions, depending heavily on informal questioning and seeking to probe and clarify until a consensus emerges.
- Staying alert to the symbolic impact of your actions and statements so a false signal is not sent which could stimulate proposals and movements in unwanted directions.
- Ensuring that all major power bases within the organization have representation in or access to top decision-makers

D-BAM: Diversity Business Alignment Maps

- Injecting new faces and new views into considerations of major changes to preclude those involved from coming to see the world the same way and then acting as systematic screens against other views.
- Minimizing political exposure on issues that are highly controversial and in circumstances where opposition from major power centers can trigger a "shootout."

The politics of D-BAM strategy implementation is especially critical when attempting to introduce a new strategy against the support enjoyed by the old strategy. Except for crisis situations where the old strategy is plainly revealed as "out-of-date", it is usually bad politics to push the new strategy through attacks on the old one. Bad-mouthing old strategy can easily be interpreted as an attack on those who formulated it and those who supported it.

It is critical to treat the past with respect. Many managers and others have been rewarded, supported, and promoted based upon their strategic actions of the past. In order to bring attention to a new strategy built for the future, you must "sell the problem, not the solution". People are usually not ready to accept strategies for problems they are not yet aware of (or are convinced they pose a threat). In other words you will need to convince others of the need for the new path based upon facts and evidence of the current or potential problem or opportunity. In this manner, they will be able

D-BAM: Diversity Business Alignment Maps

to reach the same or similar conclusion that you have reached (or at least understand how you arrived at your current point of view).

The former strategy and the judgments behind it may have been well-suited to the organization's earlier circumstances, and the people who made these judgments may still be influential. In addition, the new strategy and/or the plans for implementing it may not have been others' first choices, and lingering doubts may remain. Good arguments may exist for pursuing other actions. Consequently, in trying to surmount resistance, nothing is gained by "knocking" the arguments for alternative approaches. Such attacks often produce alienation instead of cooperation.

In short, to bring the full force of an organization behind a strategic plan integrated with Diversity and Inclusion strategies, the strategy manager must assess and deal with the most important centers of potential support and opposition to new strategic thrusts. He or she needs to secure the support of key people, co-opt or neutralize serious opposition and resistance, learn where the zones of indifference are, and build as much consensus as possible.

Strategy-Focused Organizations use the Diversity Scorecard to place and integrate strategy at the center of their management processes. They use the D-BAM to align strategic Diversity and Inclusion initiatives with the bottom-line of the business, and utilize the strategy-supportive climate and culture to serve as the

D-BAM: Diversity Business Alignment Maps

contextual glue that holds and energizes these processes for ROI-based success. The Diversity Scorecard and the D-BAM make a unique contribution by describing strategy in a consistent and insightful way. Before the development of Diversity strategy scorecards and the Diversity Business Alignment Maps, managers had no generally accepted framework for describing the impact and alignment of Diversity and Inclusion strategy on the bottom-line: They could not implement something that they couldn't describe well. So the simple act of describing strategy via the D-BAM strategy maps and Diversity scorecards is an enormous breakthrough.

This combined process produces significant performance improvements rapidly, reliably, and in a sustainable manner. The approach, while building on solid historical foundations, can be tailored to the needs of the new economy. Applying the information in this chapter will help provide a roadmap for those who wish to create their own pathway to a Strategy-Focused Diversity organization that is poised for effective execution and impact!

References

Anfuso, D., 3M Staffing Strategy Promotes Productivity and Pride" Personnel Journal, February, 1995, pp 28-34.

D-BAM: Diversity Business Alignment Maps

Baytos, Lawrence M., Designing and Implementing Successful Diversity Programs, Prentice Hall, Englewood Cliffs, New Jersey, 1995.

Byrne, J. A., "Strategic Planning", Business Week, August 26, 1996, pp. 46-52

Dennison, D. R., "What IS the Difference Between Organizational Culture and Organizational Climate? A Native's Point of View on a Decade of Paradigm Wars," Academy of Management Review, July 1996, pp 619-654.

Egan, G., "Cultivate your Culture," Management Today, April, 1994, pp. 39-42.

Gordon, G. and DiTomaso, N., "Predicting Corporate Performance and Organizational Culture", Journal of Management Studies, November, 1992, pp 783-798.

Harris, S. G. and Mossholder, K. W., "The Affective Implications of Perceived Congruence with Culture Dimensions During Organizational Transformation", Journal of Management, 1996, pp 527-548.

Hope, V. and Hendry, J. (Corporate Culture Change-Is it relevant for the organizations of the 1990's "Human Resources Management Journal, 1995, p. 61-73.

Hubbard, Edward E., "Measuring Diversity Results (MDR) Stat Pak 1: Diversity Scorecard Startup Metrics", Global Insights Publishing, Petaluma, CA, 2000.

Jacobs, R., "Corporate Reputations: The Winners Chart a Course of Constant Renewal and Work to Sustain Cultures that Produce the Very Best Products and People", Fortune, March 6, 1995, pp 54-64.

D-BAM: Diversity Business Alignment Maps

Kotter, John P. and Heskett, James L., "Corporate Culture and Performance", The Free Press, New York, NY, 1992.

McCartney, S., "Airline Industry's Top-Ranked Woman Keeps Southwest's Small-Fry Spirit Alive", The Wall Street Journal, November 30, 1996, pp B1, B11.

Sathe, Vijay, "Implications of Corporate Culture: A Manager's Guide to Action", Organizational Dynamics, Autumn, 1983.

Schein, E.H. "Culture: The Missing Concept in Organization Studies", Administrative Science Quarterly, June, 1996, p.236.

Sheridan, James E., "Organizational Culture and Employee Retention", Academy of Management Journal, December, 1992, pp 1036-1056.

Zamanou, S. and Glaser, S. R., "Moving Towards Participation and Involvement", Group and Organization Management, December, 1994, pp475-502.

Deal Terrence E. and Kennedy, Allen A., Corporate Culture Reading, Mass.: Addison-Wesley, (1982, p.4

Waterman, Jr., Robert H.., "The Seven Elements of Strategic Fit," Journal of Business Strategy 2, no.3 (Winter 1982), p. 70.

Kaplan, Robert S.; Norton, David P.. The Strategy-Focused Organization: How Balanced Scorecard Companies Thrive in the New Business Environment (Kindle Locations 117-121). Harvard Business Review Press. Kindle Edition.

Kaplan, Robert S.; Norton, David P.. The Strategy-Focused Organization: How Balanced Scorecard Companies Thrive in the New Business Environment (Kindle Locations 126-130). Harvard Business Review Press. Kindle Edition.

D-BAM: Diversity Business Alignment Maps

Kaplan, Robert S.; Norton, David P.. The Strategy-Focused Organization: How Balanced Scorecard Companies Thrive in the New Business Environment (Kindle Locations 139-146). Harvard Business Review Press. Kindle Edition.

Thompson, Jr., Arthur A. and Strickland III, A.J., "Strategy Formulation and Implementation", Irwin, Homewood Illinois, 1992.

Kaplan, Robert S.; Norton, David P.. The Strategy-Focused Organization: How Balanced Scorecard Companies Thrive in the New Business Environment (Kindle Locations 562-567). Harvard Business Review Press. Kindle Edition.

"Measures That Matter," Ernst & Young (Boston, 1998), 9. 2. Walter Kiechel, "Corporate Strategists under Fire," Fortune, 27 December 1982, 38. 3. R. Charan and G. Colvin, "Why CEO's Fail," Fortune, 21 June 1999.

Kaplan, Robert S.; Norton, David P.. The Strategy-Focused Organization: How Balanced Scorecard Companies Thrive in the New Business Environment (Kindle Locations 572-576). Harvard Business Review Press. Kindle Edition.

Kaplan, Robert S.; Norton, David P.. The Strategy-Focused Organization: How Balanced Scorecard Companies Thrive in the New Business Environment (Kindle Locations 569-571). Harvard Business Review Press. Kindle Edition.

Chapter Seven: Using a D-BAM to Become an Evidence-based Diversity & Inclusion Professional

Think back to when you first became a Diversity and/or Inclusion practitioner. Whether it was two weeks or twenty years ago, most likely the thrill and exhilaration of the career change quickly gave way to the sinking realization that implementing a Diversity and Inclusion change process is harder than it looks if you desire to make a "measurable change and impact" in the organization. Becoming an effective Diversity and/or Inclusion practitioner isn't simply a matter of years on the job. Unfortunately there are countless Diversity and/or Inclusion practitioners who have been in the job for years and are not convinced demonstrating their direct link to the bottom-line and measuring Diversity ROI impact is necessary. They have yet to master the skill set to demonstrate a basic, measurable Diversity return-on-investment (DROI®) impact of their initiatives to the C-Suite's and Board's satisfaction.

D-BAM: Diversity Business Alignment Maps

Art versus Science

Many of their approaches focus only on the "art" of the work. Although the techniques used appear factual and promise results if you use their approach, it often is not based upon real science. Instead, the approaches are based upon the practitioner's personal best practices drawn from their experience and intuition. Sometimes these methods are transferrable to you; however they can be hit or miss. Why? Because art and intuition is usually unique to an individual. Diversity and Inclusion practices that work for one Diversity practitioner in one environment may not work in another environment, let alone for another Diversity and Inclusion practitioner. Though the art and intuition of Diversity and Inclusion does have value, they can seldom be taught or transferred in a sustained, measurable way with scientific accuracy.

In contrast, Diversity and Inclusion ROI performance sciences can be taught and transferred using high performance techniques that are grounded in empirical research and demonstrated measurable evidence. A D-BAM's initiatives and impact can be monitored and tracked over time to see if the strategy produced evidence-based results. This scientific process produces a "causal chain of impact" that demonstrates how the specific Diversity and Inclusion interventions were key variables that helped generated a measurable result and outcome.

D-BAM: Diversity Business Alignment Maps

For over 30+ years I have contended that our Diversity and Inclusion field has too much "art" and not enough practices steeped in "evidence-based Diversity ROI performance sciences". I have written over 40 books; the last 15 books (including this book) are evidence and science-based Diversity ROI texts that are specifically designed to bring together a unique combination of research and empirical data to successfully prepare Diversity practitioners for the frenetic global workplace demonstrating the ROI impact of their work. Too often, I have witnessed Diversity and Inclusion departments being dismantled and cut out of the budget, not because they were not helpful, it was due to the lack of utilizing "proven Diversity sciences" that demonstrate Diversity and Inclusion's impact in evidence-based ROI and business performance terms.

What, then, does make for an effective, evidence-based Diversity and/or Inclusion practitioner? Demonstrating effective, evidence-based Diversity and Inclusion acumen is both an art and science: it results from using solid, proven, tested techniques (the "science") of Diversity ROI analytics and measurement strategies) in an inspiring and engaging way (the "art of Diversity ROI analytics and measurement strategies). Rather than advocating one specific Diversity intervention product or service, a strategy I have found worth considering is thinking about the "active science-based ingredients" that constitute an effective Diversity and Inclusion

D-BAM: Diversity Business Alignment Maps

intervention or solution you can use in the D-BAM to link to performance-based results. As a result of building your initiatives with these elements in mind, you can match and locate the most effective features in the measurement and analysis approach you are reviewing to ensure it meets your evidence-based outcome needs.

There are a huge number of Diversity, Inclusion, and Training approaches available in the marketplace. They usually try to lure you in by highlighting their ability to address a particular problem or issue the organization is facing and promise to provide you with the things you need to achieve your organizational goals. As a Diversity and Inclusion professional, the real trick however is finding the interventions or solutions that work and work consistently to drive sustainability! If you want to implement a solution or intervention that delivers a measurable Diversity ROI and/or a measurable non-financial impact, you must be able to access a decision framework that is effective and drives results. The proposed solution or intervention must be able to connect to the roots of your organization's DNA.

Checking Your Ingredients for Success

It is important to have as much detail as possible when specifying the requirements of a Diversity and Inclusion intervention or solution. Many projects run into difficulty, misunderstandings and

D-BAM: Diversity Business Alignment Maps

differences in expected outcomes because the requirements are not planned and well documented. These issues are often outlined in a Diversity and Inclusion project proposal or detailed in the project's scope documentation. Regardless of the way it is developed, the following items should be included to achieve the best chance for success. More importantly, the "Evidence-based Diversity and Inclusion professional and the evaluation project's sponsor need to reach an agreement about these key issues to create a sound strategic partnership and build accountability for the end result.

Ingredient 1: Does the Proposed Solution Include A Diagnostic Approach and Analytical Alignment Tools?

I have long advocated that "Diversity and Inclusion" should not be seen as a mere theory, but should be used as a performance improvement technology with its own set of ROI-based analytics and process improvement sciences. Driving business performance improvement requires that you have a detailed understanding of business operations and the Diversity ROI (DROI®) evaluation methodology and how it works. It begins with some initial planning, and continues with the implementation of a comprehensive data collection and evaluation process. The initial planning and analysis step is critical for generating a successful Diversity and Inclusion intervention. Many Diversity practitioners trying to develop effective business solutions find out after the fact that they should have spent more time analyzing the organization's

D-BAM: Diversity Business Alignment Maps

needs and planning the strategic linkage and alignment of the diversity initiatives that will drive the business challenges and opportunities they are trying to affect.

Ingredient 2: Does the Proposed Solution Have Objectives that are "Behaviorally Specific"?

When it comes to Diversity and Inclusion evaluation projects, there are two sets of objectives. First, there are the *objectives for the Diversity and Inclusion evaluation project itself*, indicating specifically what will be accomplished and delivered through the evaluation process. The other set of objectives are called the *Diversity and Inclusion initiative objectives* and focuses on the goals of the actual Diversity and Inclusion initiative that will be reflected in the D-BAM and ultimately add value to the organization.

Every Diversity and Inclusion evaluation project should have a major project objective and in most cases, multiple objectives. The objectives should be as specific as possible and focused directly on the Diversity and Inclusion evaluation. Sample project objectives may focus on the following outcomes:

- Determine if the Diversity and Inclusion initiative is accomplishing its objectives
- Identify the strengths and weaknesses in the Diversity and Inclusion initiative

D-BAM: Diversity Business Alignment Maps

- Determine the benefit/cost ratio and ROI of the Diversity and Inclusion initiative
- Identify who benefited the most and least from the Diversity and Inclusion initiative
- Gather data to assist in pursuing future initiatives

As the list reveals that the objectives are broad in scope, outlining from an overall perspective what is to be accomplished. The details of timing, specifications, and specific deliverables come later. The broad Diversity and Inclusion evaluation project objectives are critical because they bring focus to the project quickly and help explain the performance-driving connections shown in the D-BAM and "how" the initiatives will impact the Mission, Vision, and Key Drivers using Strategic Level Diversity and Inclusion initiatives.

Sample Hubbard D-BAM with Diversity Strategy

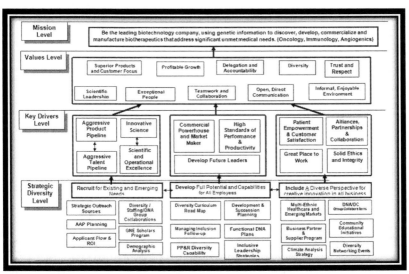

D-BAM: Diversity Business Alignment Maps

They define the basic parameters of the project and are often the beginning points of a discussion with those involved in the project.

Ingredient 3: Does the Proposed Solution Have a Clearly Defined Scope?

The scope of the Diversity and Inclusion evaluation project needs to be clearly defined. The scope can pinpoint key parameters addressed by the project. The following list shows typical scope issues that should be defined in the project:

- Target group for the evaluation
- Location of the target group
- Timeframe for the evaluation
- Technology necessary to conduct the evaluation
- Access to stakeholders
- Product line(s) to cover
- Type of Diversity process/activity/competencies being evaluated or improved
- Constraints on data collection
- Etc.

Perhaps the project is limited to certain employee or demographic groups, a functional area of the business, a specific location, a unique type of strategy, or a precise time frame. Sometimes there is a constraint on the type of data collected or access to certain individuals, such as particular customers in a targeted market

D-BAM: Diversity Business Alignment Maps

segment. Whatever the scope involves, it needs to be clearly defined in this section.

Ingredient 4: Is the Timing Clearly Defined?

Timing is critical in showing specifically "when" the Diversity and Inclusion intervention activities will occur. This means not only the timing of the delivery of the final Diversity ROI Impact study report but also the timing of particular steps and events – including when data are needed, analyzed, and reported and when presentations are made. The following list shows typical scheduled activities:

- Diversity and Inclusion initiatives and/or solutions developed
- Diversity and Inclusion Initiatives Implementation started
- Diversity and Inclusion Initiatives Implementation completed
- Start of the Diversity ROI evaluation project
- Data collection design completed
- Evaluation design completed
- Data collection begins
- Data collection completed
- Specific data collection issues (for example, pilot testing, executive interviews)
- Data analysis completed

D-BAM: Diversity Business Alignment Maps

- Preliminary results available
- Report developed
- Presentation to management

Ingredient 5: Does the Proposed Solution Spell Out the Specific Diversity and Inclusion Intervention Deliverables?

This section describes exactly what the project sponsor or client will receive when the Diversity and Inclusion intervention is completed in terms of improved competencies, reports, documents, systems, and processes. Whatever the specific deliverables, they are clearly defined in this section. Most projects will have a final report, but they often go much further, delivering new skill sets, processes and suggested methodologies for improving the Diversity and Inclusion process and/ or business issues being addressed.

Ingredient 6: Does the Proposed Solution Clearly Utilize a Proven Sciences-based Methodology and Approach?

If a specific methodology is to be used for the Diversity ROI intervention, it should be defined and state the scientific basis for its ability to obtain measurable results. A reference should be made to the appropriateness of the methodology, and how the methodology will accomplish what is needed for the Diversity and Inclusion initiative to be successful. This helps prevent initiatives that are merely "fads" that do not and cannot generate the desired

D-BAM: Diversity Business Alignment Maps

outcome. *Just because participants enjoy the intervention doesn't mean that you will have improved performance.* It must be constructed with key ingredients to achieve its behaviorally stated objectives and measurable, evidence-based outcomes. A well-designed Diversity and Inclusion intervention designed for the D-BAM can produce both: an enjoyable process and measurable results!

Ingredient 7: Does the Proposed Solution Have Clearly Defined Steps?

The specific steps which will occur should be defined showing key milestones. This provides a step-by-step understanding and tracking of the Diversity and Inclusion evaluation project such that at any given time the project sponsor or client can see not only where progress is made but also where the evaluation project is going next.

Ingredient 8: Does the Proposed Solution Spell Out the Resources Required for Success?

This section should define specific resources required to implement the intervention. This could include access to individuals, vendors, technology, equipment, facilities, competitors, or customers. All resources that may be needed should be listed along with details regarding the timing and circumstances under which the resources will be needed.

D-BAM: Diversity Business Alignment Maps

Ingredient 9: Does the Proposed Solution Highlight Fully Loaded Costs and Benefits?

The cost section details the specific costs tied to different steps of the intervention process. There is often reluctance to detail costs; however, it is important to understand the different steps of the process and their relative costs. This cost outline should also be linked to driving the organization's strategic objectives and mission. When calculating the Diversity Return on Investment (DROI®) for a Diversity and Inclusion initiative, all costs are considered. This includes not only development and implementation costs but also the costs of evaluating the program.

Ingredient 10: Does the Diversity and Inclusion Intervention Provide a Causal "Chain of Impact" to Demonstrate and Isolate Diversity's Contribution to the Results versus Other Contributors?

Eventually a Diversity and Inclusion initiative or intervention should lead to some level of impact on the organization's business. In some situations, the Diversity and Inclusion initiative is aimed at softer issues, such as improving the Diverse workforce climate, employee satisfaction, diverse customer group satisfaction, and diverse workgroup conflict reduction. In other situations, Diversity and Inclusion initiatives are aimed at more tangible issues such as cost reductions, market share, revenue improvements, productivity,

D-BAM: Diversity Business Alignment Maps

and number of voluntary turnovers, all sorted by demographic group. Whatever the case, Diversity and Inclusion initiatives and interventions should have multiple levels of objectives and must be able to demonstrate how the "specific Diversity and Inclusion intervention" drove the improvement differences and results that were achieved.

These levels of objectives, ranging from qualitative to quantitative, define precisely what will occur as a particular Diversity and Inclusion initiative is implemented in the organization. These objectives are so critical that they need special attention in their development and use. The Hubbard Diversity ROI Model® and Seven Level "Chain of Impact®" can assist in generating Diversity and Inclusion interventions with these characteristics. The complete Hubbard Diversity Return on Investment (DROI®) Methodology is taught in the Hubbard Diversity ROI Institute "Certified Diversity Return on Investment Professional (CDROI) Professional and the Certified Diversity Business Partner (CDBP) Certification training programs. A schedule of these Diversity ROI-based programs can be found using the following link:

https://attendee.gototraining.com/5975q/catalog/8188167925517902080?tz=America/Denver

D-BAM: Diversity Business Alignment Maps

or by contacting Hubbard & Hubbard, Inc. at www.hubbardNhubbardInc.com or 707-481-2268 or email: edhub@aol.com or myrahub@aol.com.

Ingredient 11: Does the Diversity and Inclusion Intervention Have a Comprehensive Data Collection Process?

Data collection is the most crucial step of the evaluation process because without data, there is no evidence of the Diversity and Inclusion initiative's impact. During the data collection process, it is necessary to determine the participant's reactions and satisfaction to the diversity initiative (Level 1), their level of learning from the intervention (Level 2), the amount of application and implementation that happened as a consequence of the diversity initiative (Level 3), the resulting business impact (Level 4), and whether the initiative generated benefits and a return on investment (Levels 5 and 6). It is necessary to collect data from at least levels 1-4 because of the chain of impact that must exist for a diversity initiative to be successfully applied into the organizational system and provide value.

To reap the benefits of the chain of impact, a key business problem that can be addressed by Diversity and Inclusion must be identified. It also requires that participants in the Diversity and Inclusion initiative experience a positive reaction to the initiative and its potential applications. They must acquire new knowledge

D-BAM: Diversity Business Alignment Maps

or skills to perform at an improved level that is a direct result of the Diversity and Inclusion intervention. As application and/or implementation opportunities arise, there should be changes in their "on-the-job" behavior that result in a measurable, positive impact on the organization. The only way to know if the chain of impact has occurred up to this point is to collect data at all four levels. The Diversity and Inclusion initiative will also generate benefits that are either quantitative or qualitative in the forms of "benefit-to-cost", dollar return-on-investment and anecdotal impacts.

An effective Evidence-based Diversity ROI initiative must be built on a comprehensive, evidence-based planning and data collection model that incorporates appropriate scientific process and critical factual information. By utilizing these science-based techniques to plan and collect data, your Diversity intervention and evaluation studies will begin on a solid foundation that positions the initiative for improved performance and organizational success!

References

Hubbard, Edward E. "Becoming an Evidence-based Diversity & Inclusion Professional", Diversity Executive Magazine, May, 2014.

Chapter Eight: A Few D-BAM Action Tools You Can Use

This chapter presents a few Action Tools (tools, templates and worksheets) you can use to support your efforts during the D-BAM creations and development process. As a strategy designer and implementer, you will have to formulate a rationale or "basis" for selecting the Diversity and Inclusion initiatives you include in your D-BAM. The tools that follow will help you utilize a logical, practical, and systems approach for selecting the Diversity and Inclusion initiatives you want to include in your D-BAM strategy.

- **HH Business Planning Template** – Facilitates detailed business planning for a Diversity and Inclusion initiative or intervention. It allows a detailed analysis of initiative target setting, organizational impact, business risk analysis, Strategic impact, Financial Impact, and Tactics Identification to implement the initiative.
- **The Diversity Measurement Planning Tree** – Highlights the alignment flow from the Organization's business objectives and its translation into Diversity and Inclusion initiatives and interventions to the Diversity and Inclusion metric and analytics to track and monitor

D-BAM: Diversity Business Alignment Maps

its progress to operationalizing the D&I initiative(s) into Action Plans to execute the D-BAM strategy.

- **Key Result Area (KRA) and Key Indicator (KI) Data Collection Worksheet** – Designed to provide a detailed approach for identifying Key Result Areas (KRA) and Key Indicators (KIs) to collect Diversity and Inclusion Data to analyze your D&I initiatives. It will also help document the specific methods which will be used to perform this data collection task and identify the Performance Targets that must be achieved to consider the initiative a success.

- **Outcome Identification Matrix** – Highlights the alignment of the Diversity and Inclusion initiative with the strategic business objectives of the organization. This allows you to assess the organization's Business Drivers and connect them to the Business Need, the Performance Need to the Potential Diversity and Inclusion Solution (your initiative) to the initiatives' expected outcome (highlighting the impact or what will change as a result of the D&I Initiative's implementation).

- **Hubbard "Five How's" Analysis for Forecasted Impact** – This tool is designed to help "reality or field-test" your Diversity and Inclusion initiatives to clearly translate how they will impact the success of the organization and drive performance to the bottom-line.

D-BAM: Diversity Business Alignment Maps

As you construct initiatives to include at the D-BAM Strategic Diversity Level, ask each of the five questions about the initiative to determine if the actions implied in the D&I initiative will result in the outcome(s) the C-Suite expects.

- **Actions and Accountability Plan** – This tool is designed to assist you in constructing a evidence-based plan to execute your Diversity and Inclusion initiative. The tool helps you capture initiative details, Tangible Business Impacts, Initiative Action Steps, Expected Results and specific Measures and Analytics to track progress and outcomes.

Hubbard & Hubbard, Inc. offers a wide range of tools, templates, worksheets, processes, webinars, automated online calculators and much more to support the D-BAM analysis, design, development, implementation, evaluation, and execution process. For further information, training program schedules, online tool access registration (with over 300 metrics; formulas, articles, downloadable forms, recorded webinars, online automated Diversity ROI Calculators, and more), contact us at **www.hubbardNhubbardInc.com**, or email us at **myrahub@aol.com** or **edhub@aol.com**, or call 707-481-2268.

D-BAM: Diversity Business Alignment Maps

Hubbard & Hubbard, Inc. Business Planning Templates

Diversity Business Plan for:

Period: _____ to _____ Date Created: _____ No. ___ of ___

Primary Contact: _____ Phone: _____

Diversity Initiative	Diversity Strategic Performance Metrics	Targets		
		FYxx	FYxx	FYxx

Organizational Impact

Business Risks

Potential Risks of Not Implementing	Potential Risks of Implementing

Strategic Impact					Financial Impact		FYxx	FYxx	FYxx
Strategic Priorities	No Impact	Little Impact	Moder-ste Impact	High Impact	Cost	Expense			
						Capital			
						FTE			
					Funding Source	Existing Resources			
						Revenue			
						Other			
						Other			
						Soft Benefits			

Tactics

FYxx	
FYxx	
FYxx	

Copyright © 2004, 2017 by Hubbard & Hubbard, Inc., International Organization and Human Performance Corporation, Petaluma, CA. All Rights Reserved. 707-763-8380 Web: www.hubbardnhubbardinc.com

D-BAM: Diversity Business Alignment Maps

Hubbard "Five How's Analysis"

Hubbard "Five How's" Analysis	
The Challenge: Innovation	**Answer:**
■ How would you know success?	■ We would do a better job of leading the market.
■ How would you know that you succeeded at leading the market?	■ We would be faster at identifying and meeting new customer needs.
■ How would you know you have succeeded at being faster at identifying and meeting new customer needs?	■ We would reduce the time it takes us to introduce new products and increase the commercial success rate of those new products
■ How would you know that you have succeeded at reducing the time it takes to introduce new products and increase the commercial success rate of those new products?	■ We will cut the time from idea to product introduction in half while doubling the commercial success rate of new products.
■ How would you know you succeeded at cutting the time frame from idea to product introduction in half while doubling the commercial success rate of new products?	■ For the next 10 ideas that get the go-ahead, we will take no more than 3 months to introduce each and at least 4 of them will be commercially successful 1 year after their introduction.

Copyright © 1999, 2014, 2017 By Hubbard & Hubbard, Inc. All Rights Reserved. Tel. 707-763-8380

Hubbard Diversity Measurement Planning Tree for _____ Company

Company Business Plan Objective:
Retain the Best & Brightest *"Retention"*

Diversity Strategic Plan Metrics

Diversity Strategic Plan Metrics:
Decrease Diverse Employee T/O by 25% by 12/31/XX by Demographic Group

Diversity Strategic Plan Metrics:
Decrease Diverse Employee T/O by 25% by 12/31/XX by Demographic Group

Diversity Strategy / Tactics

Diversity Strategy / Tactics

Diversity Strategy / Tactics
Strategy: Improved 1:1 Support for Diverse Employees
Tactic: "Mentoring"

Diversity Strategy / Tactics
Strategy: Improved 1:1 Support for Diverse Employees
Tactic: "ERG's"

Measure

Measure → Action Plans

Measure → Action Plans

Comparison: Reduction in T/O in Mentoring Group vs. Company Overall → Action Plans

- ☒ % High Potential Retention, 18-36mos
- ☒ % Critical Skills Attainment

→ Action Plans

Comparison: Reduction in T/O in ERG Group vs. Company Overall → Action Plans

- ☒ % Targeted New Hire Retention, 18-36mos
- ☒ Avg Employee Tenure by Performance Level

→ Action Plans

Page 232

D-BAM: Diversity Business Alignment Maps

Hubbard & Hubbard, Inc. Worksheets

Key Result Area and Key Indicator Data Collection Worksheet

KRAs / KIs	Methods	Performance Targets
KRA:		
KI 1:	Who:	
	How:	
	Where:	
	When:	
KI 2:	Who:	
	How:	
	Where:	
	When:	
KI 3:	Who:	
	How:	
	Where:	
	When:	
KI 4:	Who:	
	How:	
	Where:	
	When:	

Hubbard & Hubbard, Inc. Intersectional Organization and Human Performance Consulting Corporation, Petaluma, CA. (707) 763-8380.

Hubbard & Hubbard, Inc. Worksheets

Key Result Area and Key Indicator Data Collection Worksheet – Sample Items

KRAs / KIs	Methods	Performance Targets
KRA: Customer Loyalty		
KI 1: Percent rating in "satisfied" and "very satisfied" response categories on "overall customer satisfaction"	**Who:** Linda Jones **How:** Customer Service Performance Survey **Where:** Linda compiles and prints report within 7 working days of published return date of the semi-annual Customer Service Performance Survey **When:** On a semi-annual basis	Score 95% or above on this item
KI 2: Number of customer complaints resolved/total number of customer complaints	**Who:** Jerry Logan **How:** Implement new customer complaint team resolution and tracking process. Also link Key Indicator to Customer Service Performance Survey question. **Where:** Pilot in Northeast Region for 6 months and record data to report at 3 month and 6 month milestones. **When:** Report numerical progress at 3 & 6 months. Review Customer Service Performance Survey Score at 6 months	100% of customer complaints will be resolved

Definitions:

Key Result Areas (KRA): Are critical "must achieve", "make or break" performance categories for an organization. KRAs focus on an organization's outputs.

Key Indicator (KI): Is a specific measure which helps determine how well you are performing in a given KRA.

Hubbard & Hubbard, Inc. Intersectional Organization and Human Performance Consulting Corporation, Petaluma, CA. (707) 763-8380.

D-BAM: Diversity Business Alignment Maps

Outcome Identification Matrix: Aligning Business Drivers with Initiative Outcomes

Business Driver	Business Need	Performance Need	Potential Solution	Initiative Outcomes
Potential loss of market share in emerging markets and overall market performance (competition) (external driver)	To increase share of wallet in emerging markets	Increase sales force and employee knowledge of cultural competencies required to sell in emerging markets	Training on multicultural customer knowledge and buying preferences	To be able to sell against competitors' products in emerging markets To use customer cultural background information during a sales call

D-BAM: Diversity Business Alignment Maps

Action Planning Worksheet

Name:

Evaluation Period:

Action and Accountability Plan

Program:

Follow-up Date:

Tangible Business Impacts	Action Steps	Results	Measures
Specific Results Targeted for Improvement	What You are Going to Do Differently to Impact Business Results? (Actions You will take)	What will be Different If You Actually Start Taking Action? (What would we see, hear, notice is different?)	How will You Calculate the Impact of the Results? (Cost, Time, Quality, Quantity, Frequency of Occurrence-How Often)

About the Author

A Brief Bio

Dr. Edward E. Hubbard, Ph.D. is President and CEO of Hubbard & Hubbard, Inc., (for over 35 years) Petaluma, CA, an international organization and human performance-consulting corporation that specializes in techniques for applied business performance improvement, Diversity Return on Investment (DROI®) measurement and analytics, instructional design and strategic organizational development. He is the author of more than **40** Business-related books including the ground-breaking books: "The Diversity Scorecard: Evaluating the Impact of Diversity on Organizational Performance", "How to Calculate Diversity Return on Investment", "Diversity Training Return on Investment", "The Manager's Pocket Guide to Diversity Management", "The Diversity Discipline", "The Hidden Side of Employee Resistance to Change", "Mastering Secrets of Personal Success: Tools to Create the Life You Want", and many others.

Dr. Hubbard was an honoree at the Inaugural International Society of Diversity and Inclusion Professionals Living Legends of Diversity Award Ceremony in Rio Grande, Puerto Rico where he received the "Living Legends of Diversity Award" for creating the "Diversity ROI Analytics" and "Diversity Measurement Fields and

D-BAM: Diversity Business Alignment Maps

the associated Disciplines". He is one of only 18 people in the world who have received this Award.

A 1.5 Minute YouTube Introduction of Dr. Hubbard and His Diversity and Inclusion Return on Investment (DROI®) Measurement Work as a "Legend in the Diversity and Inclusion fields can be seen by Clicking the link below:

http://www.youtube.com/watch?v=ZoVqbM9wty8

Dr. Hubbard also received the "Excellence in Global Leadership Award" from the World HRD Congress as Pioneer and Founder of the Diversity ROI Analytics and Measurement fields. The highest individual professional award given.

The American Society for Training and Development (ASTD, now ATD) inducted Dr. Ed Hubbard into the prestigious "ASTD New Guard for 2003". The July/August 2007 Issue of Profiles in Diversity Journal featured Dr. Hubbard as the "Diversity Pioneer" in Diversity Measurement.

Dr. Hubbard was also awarded the 2017 Distinguished Alumni Award from The Ohio State University College of Arts and Sciences. This award recognizes an alumnus who has demonstrated distinctive achievements in a career and/or through civic involvement.

D-BAM: Diversity Business Alignment Maps

Dr. Hubbard serves on the Harvard Business Review, Diversity Executive Magazine and Strategic Diversity & Inclusion Management (SDIM) magazine Editorial Advisory Boards, and serves on the Board of Directors for The Ohio State University African American Alumni Society.

He held the position of Director, Developmental Education, The Ohio State University Newark campus and was a member of the Black Studies Department Faculty, The Ohio State University, Main Campus. Part of Dr. Hubbard's career was spent as a Lecturer at Dennison University. He also taught and worked with other Colleges and Universities here in the U.S. such as Missouri State University, Kent State University (where he serves as the Diversity Leadership and ROI Metrics Instructor for Kent's Institute for Leadership Excellence), in Canada at the University of Calgary, the U.K. at the University of Bradford in Leeds, England, the Pacific Rim, and elsewhere.

A sample of Dr. Hubbard's corporate experience includes Programming Analyst and Manager, Battelle Memorial Institute, Systems Analyst, Informatics Corporation, Systems Engineer, Xerox Corporation, Organization Development and Education Specialist, Mead Corporation, Corporate Director of Compensation, Training, Organizational Development, and Communications for the 17 Billion Dollar McKesson Corporation in San Francisco, California.

D-BAM: Diversity Business Alignment Maps

Dr. Hubbard is an expert in Organizational Behavior, Organizational Analysis, Applied Performance Improvement and ROI Measurement Strategies, Strategic Planning, Training and Development, Instructional Design, Diversity Measurement and Analytics, and Strategic Organizational Change Methodologies. He holds a Practitioner Certification and Master Practitioner Certification in Neurolinguistic Programming (NLP), a Neuroscience discipline. Dr. Hubbard earned Bachelors, Masters Degrees from The Ohio State University and earned a Ph.D. with Honors in Business Administration from Century University.

Some of Dr. Hubbard's books include the following *Best Selling* books: "The Diversity Scorecard", "How to Measure Diversity Return on Investment (DROI")", :Measuring Diversity Results", "How to Measure Diversity Training ROI", "Implementing Diversity Measurement and Diversity Management", "The Diversity Discipline", The Manager's Pocket Guide to Diversity Management", "Measuring the ROI of Employee Resource Groups and Business Resource Groups", "Diversity ROI Fundamentals", "The Hidden Side of Employee Resistance to Change", Mastering the Secrets of Personal Success, and many more books, articles, films, etc.

Other Resources

Diversity ROI Certification Institutes and Training

Hubbard Diversity ROI Institute

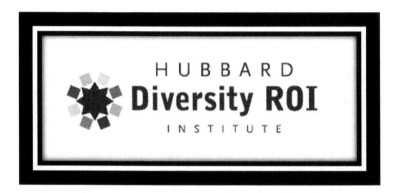

The **Hubbard Diversity ROI Institute** is the leading resource on Diversity ROI Analytics Research, Consulting, Training, and Networking for practitioners of the Hubbard Diversity ROI Methodology (DROI®). The Hubbard Diversity ROI (DROI®) Institute — is an *"applied sciences"* organization dedicated to the development of processes and methods that demonstrate Diversity's measurable value and performance improvement impact on an organization's bottom-line.

We provide **Diversity ROI Certification Training** (only available from Hubbard & Hubbard, Inc.), analytics research, consulting, benchmarking, publications and online analytical services and tools utilizing the Hubbard Diversity ROI Methodology®.

D-BAM: Diversity Business Alignment Maps

Earn Six Professional Certifications in Diversity ROI - Available ONLY from Hubbard & Hubbard, Inc.

By enrolling, you can achieve certification as a:

- Certified Diversity Trainer (CDT)
- Certified Diversity Advisor (CDA)
- Certified Diversity Performance Consultant/Technologist (CDPC)
- Certified Diversity Business Partner (CDBP)
- Certified Diversity Strategist (CDS)
- **Certified Diversity Intervention Specialist (CDIS)**

These Certifications can only be obtained from Hubbard & Hubbard, Inc. You can become Level-I up to Level III Certified in the Hubbard Diversity ROI (DROI®)Methodology

Imagine Your Name:_____, CDA, CDT (with these or other earned credentials after your name)

These certification processes are designed to help you build professional skills, knowledge and confidence to effectively improve the performance of your organization with measurable results. For example:

- **Certified Diversity Advisor (CDA)** - Perfect for Diversity Council Members and ERG/BRG Leaders and Members responsible for organizational change and

D-BAM: Diversity Business Alignment Maps

"coaching/advising" the organization through the change process. Participants are taught organizational analysis, coaching and influence skills, ROI Analysis Methods, and more.

- **Certified Diversity Trainer (CDT)** - Perfect for Internal Trainers who want to learn professional Instructional Systems Design (ISD) and Diversity Training Return on Investment (DTROI) Analysis Methods for any Diversity Training Initiative they create and implement.

- **Certified Diversity Performance Consultant / Technologist (CDPC)** - Perfect for those in an "Analyst Role" who need/want the skill set to analyze the Return on Investment impact of any Diversity Initiative they create and implement.

- **Certified Diversity Strategist (CDS)** - Perfect for those in a Diversity Leadership Role who must build Diversity Strategic Plans and Change Implementation Strategies that must demonstrate financial and other performance impacts on the organization's bottom-line.

- **Certified Diversity Business Partner (CDBP) Advanced, Senior-level (Level III) Diversity ROI Certification** - Perfect for those who need to apply Advanced ROI business and industry knowledge to partner with clients in identifying workplace and business improvement opportunities to leverage differences,

D-BAM: Diversity Business Alignment Maps

similarities and complexities for performance improvement; evaluates possible solutions and recommends solutions that will have a positive impact on performance and business results; gains client agreement and commitment to proposed solutions and collaboratively develops an overall implementation strategy that includes evaluating the ROI impact on business performance; uses appropriate cultural and inclusive interpersonal and coaching styles and other communication methods to build effective long-term relationships with the client; utilizes advanced problem-solving and data analysis and change methods to create measurable differences in the organization's performance.

- etc.

You Receive an Advanced Analysis Toolkit: Each Certification Level will enable you to leave certified to use a comprehensive toolkit of decision-support, diverse work team analysis, change management assessments, performance models, and other tools that are customized for your specific area of expertise.

D-BAM: Diversity Business Alignment Maps

Hubbard Diversity Measurement & Productivity Institute

Professional Competency-based Training and Skill-building

Although interest in measuring the effects of diversity has been growing, the topic still challenges even the most sophisticated and progressive diversity departments. Managers know they must begin to show how diversity is linked to the bottom-line or they will have difficulty maintaining funding, gaining support, and assessing progress. The **Hubbard Diversity Measurement & Productivity Institute** (HDM&P) provides on-going, solution-based skill building with a focus on measuring organizational productivity and results.

Hubbard & Hubbard, Inc. Products and Services

Products Web

www.diversitysuperstore.com

D-BAM: Diversity Business Alignment Maps

Hubbard ERG and BRG ROI Institute

ERG and BRG Training, Skill-building, and ROI Measurement Techniques for Resource Group Leaders, Sponsors, and Members

http://www.ergandbrgroiinstitute.com/

Join Us! We can help increase your Group's effectiveness and bottom line impact. As a member of the Hubbard ERG and BRG ROI Institute, you will acquire expert ROI (Return on Investment) services and ERG and BRG support resources. Our ERG and BRG Institute team of experts will provide critical advice, tools, templates and processes that produce a value-added ROI impact for all of your initiatives.

Let us help you create an entire ERG and BRG strategy and ERG and BRG process from concept to delivery, as we have for many Fortune 500™ and Fortune 100™ companies around the world.

D-BAM: Diversity Business Alignment Maps

We can help you measure the Return on Investment (ROI) impact of any Employee Resource Group's (ERGs) and Business Resource Group's (BRGs) initiative as well as any other initiatives, goals and strategies.

As a member, you will have access to ERG/BRG focused surveys, member development tools, automated ROI calculators, worksheets, templates, case studies, over 300 formulas, and much, much, more!

Metriclink Dashboard and Scorecard Services

MetricLINK®

Comprehensive Online Performance Measurement and Management Services for Organizational Excellence

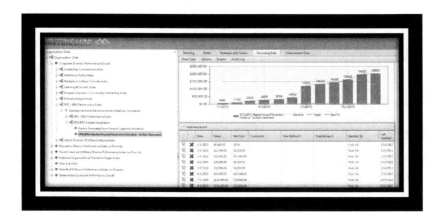

D-BAM: Diversity Business Alignment Maps

Now you can develop, track, analyze and report your ERG and BRG ROI initiatives using a state-of-the-art online service that was designed with ERGs and BRGs in mind. Practical and easy-to-use, this service gives your group an advanced project planning and Diversity ROI analytics tool to demonstrate your strategic bottom-line impact in data based, financial terms.

Performance Spotlights and Publishing Opportunities

As a member of the Hubbard ERG and BRG Institute, your ERG/BRG efforts can be showcased. Our Performance Spotlights (PS) is a place where Hubbard ERG and BRG Institute members can find ERG/BRG stories of success, learn how a challenge was addressed, or how an ERG/BRG was utilized for performance improvement.

It is a place where we spotlight and provide you with a strategy, tool, or tip. We can highlight the success of your efforts and enroll your Group's *ROI case study* and work in our **ROI Awards and Recognition Program** and/or **Publish Your Case Study in a Diversity ROI Casebook.** If you would like to discuss a potential case study for publication, please contact us.

D-BAM: Diversity Business Alignment Maps

Measuring ROI of Diversity Initiatives, ERG/BRG Initiatives, and Other Webinars

We provide members with "tool-based" Webinars on a variety of subjects that are important to your group's growth and development. Check our site at www.hubbardnhubbardinc.com, and/or http://www.ergandbrgroiinstitute.com/ under "Institute Events" for current details and programming. Our goal is to provide you and your group with resources and tools that help you drive measurable ROI-based performance that increases you success!

We can be reached by email message using the following link http://www.ergandbrgroiinstitute.net/Business-Resource-Group-Saint-George-UT.html or Call: **(855) 443-9147,** we are happy to help.

Index

"

"V" Model, 148

3

3M
application of successful innovation culture, 184

A

ability to execute strategy
critical importance of, 175
Achieving strategic alignment
questions to ask, 165
Action Tools
tools, templates, worksheets to support D-BAM, 227
Actions and Accountability Plan worksheet, 229
active science-based ingredients
to impact the bottom-line, 213
alignment and linkage, 100
Alignment Process, 104
art and intuition
versus the "science" of Diversity and Inclusion, 212
ATD
formerly ASTD, 63

B

Building a Spirit of High Performance, 191
Building a Strategy-Supportive Corporate Culture, 179
Building and Implementing "Solution-Centered" Diversity Strategies, 32
Building Centers of Diversity Excellence, 87
Business Alignment Matrix, 151

C

cause-and-effect logic, 39
Certifications in Diversity ROI, 242
Certified Diversity Business Partner, 223

D-BAM: Diversity Business Alignment Maps

Certified Diversity Return on Investment Professional, 223

champions
  examples of ways to reward them, 192

combined spending power of individual racial groups, 71

corporate culture
  definition of, 182

Cost of Not utilizing Diversity and Inclusion, 73

create excellence in performance
  using Diversity, 92

Creating the fit between Strategy and Culture, 187

creating value from intangible assets, 35

C-Suite, 3, 4, 5, 15, 63, 118, 146, 211, 229

D

Data collection
  process of, 224

D-BAM, 4, 5, 18, 23, 45, 46, 48, 49, 55, 56, 62, 63, 99, 100, 101, 103, 108, 109, 111, 117, 124, 125, 132, 133, 134, 135, 136, 137, 138, 139, 143, 145, 152, 154, 156, 157, 158, 159, 160, 161, 162, 163, 164, 165, 166, 167, 170, 171, 177, 181, 184, 187, 196, 199, 205, 206, 211, 212, 214, 216, 217, 221, 227, 228, 229

Dealing with Company Politics
  strategies you can use, 202

Diversity
  as a competitive advantage, 67
  four dimensions of Diversity, 64

Diversity and Inclusion certifications, 111

Diversity and Inclusion ROI performance sciences, 212

diversity as a strategic asset, 57

Diversity Business Alignment Map, 4, 18, 45, 55, 100, 121, 139, 154, 155, 156

Diversity Business Alignment Maps, 1, 2, 3, 15, 31, 45, 48, 49, 207

Diversity Leadership Commitment, 102, 103

D-BAM: Diversity Business Alignment Maps

Diversity Links to Productivity and Performance, 75
Diversity management
definition of, 64
diversity measurement
characteristics of skilled professionals, 93
Diversity ROI, 5, 99, 109, 111, 112, 113, 116, 118, 119, 131, 132, 133, 134, 135, 137, 138, 139, 140, 143, 146, 151, 152, 153, 169, 172, 211, 213, 214, 215, 219, 220, 223, 225, 237, 238, 240, 241, 242, 243, 248
Diversity ROI (DROI®), 241
Diversity ROI Analytics, 241
Diversity Scorecard, 38, 45, 51, 60, 112, 154, 155, 156, 158, 159, 160, 161, 162, 163, 164, 165, 166, 167, 169, 170, 171, 174, 206, 208, 237, 240
Diversity's Contribution
business contributions of, 84
diversity-maturity
characteristics of, 88

E

Edward E. Hubbard, 1, 2, 60, 168, 237
enjoy the intervention
fun vs. improved performance, 221
enterprise-wide strategy map, 121, *See* also generic strategy map
evidence-based, 213
Evidence-based Diversity and Inclusion professiona, 215
execution process
why strategies don't work, 49
experience of Inclusion, 127

F

Fostering Champions
ways to develop them, 201

G

generic strategy map, 24

H

HH Business Planning Template, 227
Hubbard "Five How's" Analysis for Forecasted Impact worksheet, 228

D-BAM: Diversity Business Alignment Maps

Hubbard Diversity Measurement & Productivity Institute, 245
Hubbard Diversity Measurement and Productivity (HDM&P) Institute, 61
Hubbard Diversity Return on Investment Methodology, 152, 153
Hubbard Diversity ROI Institute, 241

I

impact of diversity on the bottom line
  examples of, 81
Importance of Business Alignment, 146
interpreting organizational culture
  model of Vijay Sathe Harvard, 183

J

Judith Rosner, 59

K

Key Result Area (KRA) and Key Indicator (KI)

Data Collection Worksheet
worksheet, 228

L

Lawrence Bayos, 65
learning and growth perspective, 29, 30, 47, 123, 142, 144
Linking Intangibles to Value Creation, 27

M

Manifestations of Culture
  examples of, 182
Marilyn Loden, 59
MBWA
  definition of, 198
Measurement Environment, 135
Metriclink Dashboard and Scorecard Services, 247
Mission, Vision, and Key Drivers
  a D-BAM with strategic content, 217

N

needs analysis, 114, 116

D-BAM: Diversity Business Alignment Maps

O

Organizational culture
definition of, 181
Outcome Identification Matrix, 228

P

Productivity, 79

R

R. Roosevelt Thomas, 59
Retention, 77

S

Senior Management' Overall Role, 154
Seven Level "Chain of Impact®, 223
Six objectives
   consistent in Strategy Maps and Scorecards, 144
Steps in Strategic Thinking, 21
strategic business partner, 4, 53, 61, 63
strategic business partners, 95
strategic thinker
   Characteristics of, 19
Strategic thinking, 16, 17, 21
strategy, 16
Strategy
   A Step in a Continuum, 43
   Applied Definition of, 25
strategy manager
   undertanding the power structure, 203
Strategy maps
   Why they are important, 42
Strategy Maps
   Definition of, 23
strategy-implementers, 189, 190, 196
Strategy-Supportive Climate, 196
strong and distinctive culture
   action steps to build successful culture, 184

T

The Diversity Measurement Planning Tree
template model, 227
transitional model
   compensation rewards structure, 168
Translating Mission into Desired Outcomes, 44
typically define their diversity
   Typical definition of Diversity, 54

U

ultimate success

D-BAM: Diversity Business Alignment Maps

Importance of
DiversityROI, 131
Utilizing strategy, 16

V

Value Creation, 4, 30, 121, 125, 131, 139

Value Creation through Intangible Alignment with Strategy, 30

W

Webinars, 249